NO BLOOD IN THE TURNIP
Memoirs of a Codependent

Maple Sudds

Published by BookLocker.com, Inc., St. Petersburg, Florida.

Printed on acid-free paper.

BookLocker.com, Inc.
2018

First Edition

In Memoriam

Essie Dell Sudds English, my birth mother and my father, George Written. Olivia Singletary Written, my paternal grandmother. I would like to acknowledge the memory of those individuals who helped shape my life growing up. Also, in remembrance of Reverend C.L. Townsel who was my landlord.

In memory of my beloved pastor Reverend Murphy Lee Hunt; his patience and endurance with my dysfunctional family went above and beyond. I have now realized that we put his calling to the test. Pastor Hunt was truly a phenomenal man of God to have dealt with *my family and me!* Rev. Dr. Murphy L. Hunt will be greatly missed, cherished, and remembered always.

This book is dedicated to my two sons
and
My African-American Community

Author's Note

In 1989, when I first started writing my story, it was cathartic. I spent every waking morning from 2:00 a.m. until 4.00 a.m. writing about pent-up emotions that were tormenting me. I feel that writing about my emotions helped me narrowly escape the psychiatric ward. I could not grasp how my life had gotten all screwed-up. I now realize that in everyone's life there is a journey. Because of bad choices, some of our journeys are long and difficult; experience brings about a change in our lives. I believe we have to learn and grow with different experiences at our own pace. Perhaps my life experiences were no mistake; it was just my path. Surviving the trials, tribulations and hardships that confronted me, I can now look back and say, "Oh! if it wasn't for Amazing Grace!"

To my readers, this story has profanity and the N—word. I apologize for the offensive language, but in keeping with the true essence of the events that occurred, I feel that it is important to convey to YOU the real feelings and meaning of this narrative depiction of my codependent life. Some names have been changed in order to protect the privacy of the various individuals involved. Thank you for allowing me to tell my story in a raw and compelling way.

CONTENTS

FOREWORD

The old saying, "You can't get blood from a turnip," characterizes something that is extremely difficult. Maple is a woman who has lived an interesting, though challenging life. I met her one evening while she was babysitting for a family member. Her inner strength and spiritual countenance was evident in her quiet demeanor, and in the wisdom of her eyes.

Life was not easy for her. As I read the draft of *No Blood in the Turnip*, I was reminded of one of my favorite poems, "Mother to Son", by author Langston Hughes, in which a mother tells her boy that "Life for me ain't been no crystal stair." Maple's life was like that. She tried to control the situations and people around her, but it was not an easy task – actually it was impossible. As she struggled through life, she looked for any crevice or hand-hold to hang on or climb up, and she never gave up.

Maple began to keep a journal of her actions and her thoughts. This book, *No Blood in the Turnip*, is comprised of her life events, trials, and her tribulations. The book reads like snapshots taken in random sequence; each snapshot gives a bit of history, a lot of emotion, and the story of a woman who just keeps on trying to make things better.

Not to say that Maple was always perfect; it just isn't possible to survive the streets of Mooretown without a bit of anger, fear, and manipulation. When her whole world seemed to be slipping away, she tried to control, to "patch," and hold on too tightly. She had a picture in her mind of the life she wanted for her family, but the men in Maple's life were not always easy to deal with and, not always helpful as fathers, husband and sons. She fought so hard to save her marriage, and to keep her sons from the dangers of drugs and life on the streets. She tried to lead and control their paths, but it was not meant to be.

This book is also a testimony to faith--a reminder that God is always with us. Sometimes, the only light in the darkness is the one that comes from faith. God always gave Maple "just enough light for the steps she was on." His voice was heard in the darkest moments. Her relationship with Jesus, her church community, and her family kept her going when many other people would have given up on themselves and others.

This book is filled with hope that her sons still have the opportunity for better lives that are productive and blessed. With this book, Maple shares her story and her healing. She hopes that others faced with similar trials will learn from her mistakes and make wise choices. She wants other women to find their faith, develop their talents, and learn to live without destructive relationships.

I hope you enjoy reading *No Blood in the Turnip* as much as I did.

Sharon P. Burford
Professional School Counselor
Shreveport, Louisiana

Introduction

In the Black Baptist church where I grew up, the older folks would say, "Chile, if you got that old-time religion, you ought to show *some* sign!" When that old Baptist preacher would deliver his sermons or the choir would sing, there wasn't enough ushers to assist those shouting sisters. Their shouts and praises were because they were saved, sanctified, and filled with the Holy Ghost. But since I've become an adult, got married, and had children, I have often wondered if all those old shouting sisters' tears and emotional outbursts were because they had had the "holy ghost," or from all the burdens they were bearing. Most times, for many years, my Sunday mornings' emotional outbursts didn't have anything whatsoever to do with the Holy Ghost: tears and outbursts were from frustration, desperation, and depression. Life had turned on me, and I had retreated into my own little world of self-pity, anger, and resentment.

The late 80's were dark years of despair. There were times I had panic attacks while driving down the interstate, and Lord, don't let a car horn blow! I'd about jumped out of my skin—I was a nervous wreck! I couldn't understand why my life was in such shambles: why I believed lies and then felt betrayed, why I spent most of my life trying to control my husband, and worrying that my sons would be like him, and why I remained in a destructive marriage that wasn't working? I eventually felt abandoned by God.

But, by the year of 1993, from my life experiences, I felt that I had been through the *fire* and come out pure *gold*. I knew what life was all about, and had the capability to help someone else. I decided to become a part-time drug counselor. Yep! That was my calling—a drug counselor. So, I enrolled in a twelve-week drug counseling course that was being offered through AT&T, the company with which I was employed.

In the classroom, there were about fifteen students, and everyone had their own personal stories of addictions. After having heard all their stories, I couldn't identify with any of them. I felt that I was the only "normal" one there. I had never been drunk, never done drugs, never smoked, gambled, nor shoplifted. I realized drug counseling was not my calling, and I felt an air of self-righteousness, because I wasn't like "those" people. I did not have a disorder, because my life had been centered on my family, church, and being a "good" Christian.

On that first Saturday morning, the facilitator had pointed to me and said, "Now, young lady, it's your turn to introduce yourself, and tell us why you chose this course."

I stood up tentatively. "My name is Maple," I said, "but my nickname is Georgann. I want to become a drug counselor so that I can help people."

"Have you personally had any problem with addiction?" asked the facilitator.

"No, but I know how devastating it can be, because my husband made my life a pure hell!" My heart pounded. *Oh Lord! Please don't let me start crying.*

"Would you like to talk about it?" said the facilitator. "We're all here to learn from each other. Everyone else shared their stories, so now we would like to hear yours."

I shared my story.

"Maple," said the facilitator, "did you ever attend an Al-Anon meeting?"

"No, but twice I attended a family group meeting. When my youngest son was in rehab, I attended the After-Care program."

"You could really benefit from Al-Anon. The program helps families and friends deal with the effects of alcoholism, drug addictions, and other compulsive disorders that their loved one has," said the facilitator.

"I don't need to attend no Al-Anon program!" I snapped. "My life is fine now, 'cause that's all in the past."

"The reason I suggested Al-Anon is because you seem to be carrying some emotional baggage. I believe strongly that the Al-Anon program would benefit you more so than counseling classes."

My face frowned, "Emotional baggage?!!" I repeated.

"Yes Maple. While you were telling about your life experiences with your family, you had such a dazed look about your face, and the tears spilled from your eyes."

"Well, if you've been through what I've been through, you would cry too!"

"Did you ever go to therapy, seeking counseling?"

"No."

"Maple, that tells me that you have not recovered from your experiences. Before you can help someone else, you need to be in a recovery program for yourself."

One of the other students spoke up. "From what you said, you were an enabler to your family."

I could feel the blood creeping up in the back of my neck. "How did I enable them? I was doing my part as a wife and mother." I continued, "I did everything that I could possibly do to help them and get them to do what was right! But nothing worked."

"Maple," she said, "your help was destructive. That's what an enabler is. It is a destructive form of helping others. You said that if your husband didn't pay the bills, you would pay them. That was not helping him. That was being an enabler to his addiction."

"Well, somebody had to keep a roof over our heads and put food on the table. I wasn't gon' let *my* children starve!"

"Maple, wouldn't you feed him when he didn't help financially, thinking that he would do better the next payday?"

I was getting confused. But I was not ready to concede, because I *knew* I did not have a problem.

"Maple, aren't you in denial?" she asked. I could feel my face getting flushed. I swirled in my seat as one student after another put their two cents in, whereby I was getting angrier and angrier, until the little hairs on the back of my neck were sticking out. I wanted to yell out, "Why are y'all dumping on me?" I thought *they just want to dump on me because I'm not like them. I don't have no addiction!*

"Okay, class," said the facilitator, "that's enough about Maple. There are two books that are a requirement for this class, and they are *The Boy Who Couldn't Stop Washing* by Judith L. Rapoport M.D., and *Codependent No More* by Melody Beattie."

All that next week I dreaded the weekend. Ten o'clock Saturday morning I sat in the classroom with my two new required books.

"I see everyone got their books." The facilitator held *Codependent No More.* "Those of you who have heard about or read this book raise your hands."

Every ones' hands went up except mine.

The facilitator said, "Maple, this book could really be helpful to you. Are you familiar with the word codependent?"

My heart sunk, knots formed in my stomach. *Oh Lord,* I thought, *here they go, ready to dump on me again. I'll be so glad when this class is over. One thing I know, I will* **never** *take another class on addiction!*

"I vaguely recall hearing it," I answered. "But what does that have to do with me? I'm not codependent!" I snapped.

Another student spoke up. "Yes, but Maple...didn't you say that on Fridays you would go looking for your husband, and sometimes you would send your older son to look for him too?"

"Yes I did, because we needed his money to help with those bills. And how does sending my son to look for his father have anything to do with being codependent?"

"Maple, that's one of the codependent characteristics, trying to control another human being at any extreme."

I became very defensive. It seemed like I was being accused of being a bad mother. Through the remainder of the course, my lips were zipped when it came to discussing my personal life, and I became closed minded to theirs. I viewed them as perpetrators; recovering addicts, trying to make amends for all the damages they had done to "innocent" victims, like me. With my smug attitude, I participated enough to pass the course. Then I put the two books that I never actually read on my shelf, to collect dust.

Fast-forward to 2003. I had been writing and rewriting my life story. I was still attending church, and on at least one Sunday morning I stood before my church congregation crying and asking for prayer for my oldest son because of a disturbing dream. I had thought that I had put those emotional displays behind me, but I was still puzzled as to why both my sons went in and out of jail like a revolving door, and wondering why they just couldn't get their lives together.

Friends would say to me, "It's not your fault your sons turned out to be that way, because it's a known fact that you brought them up in the church. You did everything that a mother could possibly do in bringing them up right. But, you got to remember, they have their father's genes too. And you know all those male Dunbars stay in jail." I wanted to believe that was the case. But something inside of me just wouldn't accept it. There had to be a logical explanation other than, "They are just like their father and his brothers."

Not getting any answers to my satisfaction, I remembered the book the facilitator had suggested that I read, *Codependent No More* by Melody Beattie. I took it off the shelf and started reading, this time with an open mind. Once I began to read, the word "codependent" came alive, took on legs, wrapped around my brain, squeezed my intelligence and screamed, "Hey! That's you." Wow! What an eye-opener. I was astounded as I read page after page, I couldn't read fast enough! I turned the next page. I read. I began to understand and make the connection. As I continued reading, so much was revealed to me. I couldn't cram it all in. I was in amazement. All the examples and illustrations being given in that book, just as the facilitator and the students had tried to convey to me years ago, when I wasn't ready to face the truth were there before me, jumping out of the pages...my life!

In Beattie's book, she defines a codependent as one who has let another person's behavior affect him or her, and who is obsessed with controlling that person's behavior. Beattie defines Codependency as those self-defeating learned behaviors that the codependent develops. Codependents look strong, but feel helpless. Codependent people are controllers, but in reality are being controlled themselves. Codependents are also caretakers, rescuers, and enablers, and they live in denial. Beattie says the codependents rescue people from their responsibilities, by taking on their responsibilities for them, and that codependents behaviors, like so many self-destructive behaviors, become habitual. She says "Having these problems does not mean that we are bad, defective, or inferior. We have just been doing the wrong things for the right reasons. Some of us learned these codependent behaviors as children, some as adults. We may have learned some of these behaviors from our interpretation of religion. Most codependents developed these behaviors out of necessity to protect ourselves and meet our needs." As I read and read, I was blown away. I thought, *Oh, my Jesus! This could be written as my epitaph: HERE LIES MRS. CODEPENDENT! SHE WAS A CONTROLLER, ENABLER, RESCUER, AND LIVED IN DENIAL!*

Reading Beattie's book compelled me to have a reality check; how the effect of my codependency behaviors had been a contributing factor in the failures of my sons. I had never wanted to take any ownership in that, because I had done what the Bible said about training up a child in the way that they should go. I took my children to church every Sunday. But my conscience spoke, "Yes, but what were they witnessing at home? Had their home life been a good example?"

Then, Dr. Phil, the therapist, with his philosophy of "When parents fight before their children, it writes on the slate of who they are," just added salt to my wound that had never healed. The fussing, cursing, and fierce confrontations before my sons were not training up a child in the way that he "should" go. But it had everything to do with the way that he "would" grow. I had to face reality; my sons were raised in a destructive home environment. Not only was that brought to the open, I was forced to recognize something else Dr. Phil said: "Sometimes we create the very thing that we fear." My greatest fear had been that my sons would become more Dunbar statistics.

Why wasn't there a Dr. Phil Television Show years ago? Would I have been receptive? Or would I still have been in my closed-minded view, "the victim"? I never realized that we all were victims, especially my sons. I've found that many in my African-American community, like myself, are not familiar with the word "codependent." Nor do we realize the effect that a negative home environment plays in our children's lives. So, I hope I don't offend my African-American community as I speak from my heart and ask these questions: Why are the juvenile detention facilities housing so many of our children? Why do our children have the largest rate of school drop outs of all races? Why are an estimated 12.6 percent of black men in their late 20s in jail or prison? What is the root of their problems? Maybe, like my sons, some grew up in a destructive home environment. Our children pay the price long, long afterward. It damages their lives. It wounds their spirits.

Granted, I realize other races have some of the same issues. But by opening up my soul and mind, I am learning, and I have learned so much. I like to share what I've learned to help others—especially *my* people. And to use my life story as an example for others not to make the same mistakes that I've made. I implore you, read my story with an open mind. Inspect it, dissect it, and pick it apart. Make your analysis. In the process, perhaps you will see yourself in my story. Our children are to be our finest fruits, and we, the parents, are to be their role models. But sometimes our children are contaminated by the very ones that are supposed to be their nurturers.

Chapter 1
Unwanted Child

Where is Carl? Why didn't he come home last night?

I stood at my bedroom window, a cup of Folger's in my hand, looking out on the dark street. I could see the signal light at the corner of West 70th and Pines Road, and the Circle K store, where a few early morning customers were going in and out.

Lord! Where is he?

My son and I lived in a two-bedroom apartment on the west side of Shreveport. We moved here after Carl's father and I separated. I thought if we got a fresh start in a quiet neighborhood, things would be different. But things had not changed with Carl. If anything, they had gotten worse. My baby boy had never stayed away from home all night.

The sudden blast from the radio's alarm startled me. *It was time to get ready for work.* The warm water of my morning shower was inviting, but I could not relax. My face was drawn, nothing unusual. Worrying, a tight chest, feelings of defeat—these were as normal for me as breathing.

I went to my closet, grabbed a blouse, and a pair of blue jeans, while contemplating whether to go to work, or go searching for Carl. *Lord, where would I start?*

The 6 a.m. news report blasted through my thoughts.

"Last night, around 11 p.m., a murder was committed during an attempted armed robbery at an automated teller machine. The police have apprehended an 18-year-old black male suspect whose name is Carl Dunbar."

I felt as if I'd had a blow to the stomach. My heart stopped. *No! No! Not Carl! He would never do such a thing!*

It was unthinkable, Carl in jail for murder! Now both my sons are incarcerated!

I sank down in the brown leather recliner I'd had more than a decade. Over and over again I had patched that old chair with duct tape, attempting to make it last. I had tried to fix it, as I had tried to fix my marriage and my children.

Just two weeks before, I'd had a talk with God concerning Carl. I told God that I had done all that I knew to do, and I could not think of anything more. I was so tired, that I surrendered my son... I placed Carl in the Lord's hands.

I felt the tears streaming down my face. I angrily wiped them away, while thinking, *Girl, get real! You should be tough by now.*

With all the disappointments I've been through, one would think that I should be stronger. But how can I keep from crying after hearing that my son has committed murder? I just wanted to bury my face in Mama's big shoulders and cry: "Where have I gone wrong in raising my sons?" It seemed my life had been nothing but turmoil after turmoil, as I retraced my history:

Essie Dell Sudds, my birth mother was from a small town called Mansfield, Louisiana, about fifty miles south of Shreveport. She'd had one teenage pregnancy and left the child to be raised by her aunt. At the age of seventeen, she arrived in Shreveport to live with her Uncle and his wife, in search of a better life. But she met my daddy who, at the age of nineteen, already had a reputation, being called "Sweet George" by his peers. Essie Dell was vulnerable and fell for his cunning ways. She became pregnant, once again. My daddy joined the Navy, escaping his responsibility of fatherhood. So, Daddy's mother took Essie Dell in. And on that cold and wintry night of December 5, 1944, at Charity Hospital, I was born, and given the name, Maple.

Months later, with all the uncertainty in her life, not having any means to support herself and a newborn baby, Essie Dell struck out on her own, leaving me with my paternal grandmother. Daddy's mother felt I resembled her son too much not to have his name, so she nicknamed me Georgann.

My grandmother, Olivia, (whom I called Mama) was my pillar of strength in her 5 feet, 8 inches, 280-pound frame. Mama had little formal education, just the basics of reading, writing, and arithmetic that she needed to be independent. She was a strong-willed woman who was determined to make it on her own, but our economic condition was somewhat depressed. Mama could barely find part-time maid work. Mama's daughter, Aunt Ophelia, and son, Uncle Robert, helped financially whenever they could, but both had families of their own. After a two-year stint in the Navy, Daddy returned home. Mama thought those difficult days would be better. However, as Mama was sitting at the kitchen table with a hand full of unpaid bills, a frown and worried look appeared on her moon-shaped face.

"Whatcha doin', Mama?" I asked.

"Tryin' to figure out how I'm gonna pay all these bills. The rent is due, the light bill is due, and the gas and water bill too!" Mama gave a heavy sigh. "Somethin' gonna go unpaid this month, 'cause we *gotta* eat. And there jus' ain't a nuff money to go 'round!"

Daddy, who was getting dressed for a night on the town, seemed oblivious to Mama's distress. Angry and frustrated, Mama said, "George, you 'bout the most *triflin'* son I got! You know you need to git a full-time job and help me take care of yo' daughter!"

That really struck a nerve with Daddy. Something was said that no child should ever hear from a parent. It would forever be engraved in my memory.

"Georgann is you and Ophelia's responsibility!" Daddy's boisterous voice yelled. "I didn't ask you to raise her. That was you and Ophelia's doings. I was away fighting for my country and sending money home to you every month to save for me!" Daddy continued angrily, "When I came home, all that money I sent to you was gone!"

Mama jumped out of her chair like she had been struck by a bolt of lightning. Her fiery red eyes looked like she wanted to slap the *black* off Daddy. She yelled, "George! Don't you *speak* to me in dat tone of voice! 'Cause I'll knock the *hell* outta you! Anyway, yo' sister Ophelia caint have chilluns, so she begged and pleaded wit me to adopt Georgann, 'cause she promised me dat she was gonna help take care of her."

Daddy bugged his big eyes. "You mean to tell me, you let somebody like Ophelia talk you into adoptin' Georgann?"

"Yes, George!" snapped Mama.

"How could you have listened to what Ophelia says? Ophelia's brains slow as molasses." Daddy continued, "Any woman that marries a widower with eight children ain't too *bright*!"

"We tried to do what we thought was best for the baby. Bonse {being} you left the po' gurl pregnant wit' yo' baby, and somebod' had to help her!"

Daddy, speaking in a lower tone of voice, snapped, "Well, you could have helped her, but not take the baby to raise!"

Of course, those words spoken in my presence left me with even more mixed emotions. Love and resentment battled, and fear screamed that if something ever happened to my Grandmama, I wouldn't have anyone.

Shreveport, Louisiana is my family's home, in a neighborhood called Mooretown. The community was named after a colored man who taught school and invested his money in real estate. Mooretown was a community built for colored people. The majority of the citizens were hard working, God-fearing people just like any of the other colored sections of the city. For the most part, however, Mooretown was viewed by some as the roughest and toughest section of town.

Mooretown's thoroughfare streets were Hollywood, Broadway, and Jewella. On the southeast edge of Mooretown, on Hollywood, in a small corner area, right behind a funeral home named Winnfield was a community called Stills Quarters, where my family lived. It was a community with just two streets, Faye and Sanders. The streets began at Jewella and ended at the railroad tracks. Both streets had a mixture of regular style houses and those "post-civil war" shotgun houses. Shotgun houses consisted of three rooms; the front room, a middle room and the kitchen. You could look from the front door clear through to the back door. Everyone knew their neighbors, and the people were friendly.

On the corner of Sanders Street and Jewella Avenue was the home of my grandmother's parents, O.C. and Era Singletary, but they were called Papa Tave and Mama Puddin'. It was a white frame house with three bedrooms. There was a long porch extending to both ends of the house, with a well-used wooden swing on the end. Large trees enveloped the dwelling, giving plenty of shade in the summer. It was considered the family house, and we fondly called it the Big House.

In my young mind, I couldn't imagine what place could be better than the Big House! It is where I have my fondest memories of those Heaven and Hell parties and Saturday fish dinners…fund raising events pertaining to the church. The big house is where I learned to always respect my elders. But, it is also where, when I was around five years old, I watched the hearse carry Papa Tave's body away. The big house is where I was taught to always respect the work of God.

Even to this day, I can still hear the urgency in Mama Puddin's voice. Quickly, she would order, "Gal, go fetch me dat quilt 'hind dat kitchen do'! Make haste!" The clap of thunder and the flashing of lightning brought fear on her face.

"Whatcha gonna do wit'da quilt, Mama Puddin'?"

"We gon' cover dat mirror 'fore lightnin' strike it!"

"How lightnin' gonna strike a mirror?"

"Gal, don't you know anythang? Mirrors draw lightnin'! Now hush and be quiet!"

Everyone's hands were busy, hurriedly covering mirrors, unplugging all the electrical appliances and turning off lights. Silently, we sat in the dark, and the only visible sights were flashes of lightning and the "white" of our eyeballs. Mama Puddin' said in a frightened voice, "When God is doin' His work, we had betta show some respect!"

Hearing about God has been a part of my life, all my life. My family was not educated, but they were God-fearing folks. Morning Star Baptist Church is a legacy that Mama Puddin' and others had organized in 1929. The church originated in a shotgun house in Stills Quarters. Years later, that old white wood-frame church building set on the corner of Hollywood and a street named Lucille, held many memories, especially those first Sunday night Communion Services. I was fascinated when Reverend Henry Woodson, who had a big head and a stocky body, stood in the pulpit, where he became so involved and demonstrative with his sermons that his hand gestures and body movements were both frenetic and evocative. I found myself unconsciously weaving and bobbing my head, captivated by his every movement.

The older folks would always say, "The Holy Ghost struck like lightnin' and burned like fire!" Reverend Woodson had that powerful voice and the movements that could deliver meat to his flock as he said, "They led Jesus from judgment hall to judgment hall. And my Jesus never said a mumbling word!" Reverend Woodson's big white handkerchief would represent the cross that Jesus carried. He would throw the handkerchief across his shoulder, pull on his ear and give a hooplike sound. That's when the Holy Ghost showed up. Members were shouting, running in the aisles, and falling out. If there wasn't any *smelling salt* to revive the semiconscious member, their shoe would be put to their nose for resuscitation! Those electrifying services would have my eyes gazing, from one to the other. They were having a Hallelujah good time!

My grandmother's family took much pride in saying they were born again Christians and filled with the Holy Ghost. Their faith was unquestionably strong. They supported the church dutifully, loved visits from the preachers, and practiced being their neighbor's helper. But, not only did they have faith in God, they also had a belief in something else.

Mama's youngest sister, Nannie, whose personality was as feisty as she was black, was my favorite great-aunt. Her tall and straight framed appearance was that of a strong and healthy woman, but she loved those Pall Mall cigarettes, and she always had a nagging cough. Nannie, who was once married to a man named Jessie, was the designated cook and housekeeper for the Big House. However, some days, she could be found lying in bed with some sort of complaint.

"Mama, why is Nannie always sick?" I asked.

Mama's body stiffened with anger. "Dat low-down bastard hoodooed my baby sister!" she said, "and dat's why she caint hold a job. Cause she stays *sick* all the time!"

"Mama, what's hoodoo?"

"You're too young to know, chile."

"Well, why would Uncle Jessie do bad thangs to Nannie?"

"He jus' low-down and dirty, dat's why! He didn't want Nannie and didn't want nobod' else to have her either." Mama continued, "Nannie was on the brink of death, and the doctor couldn't find out what was wrong wit her, but we got her some help jus' in time."

"Who helped her, Mama?"

Mama spat tobacco juice in her spit-cup, then said, "Baby, I shouldn't be tellin' this, but someday you might find out 'bout it anyway. So, I might as well tell you now." Mama paused a minute, then spoke. "We took Nannie to Powhatan, Louisiana, 'bout sixty miles south of here, to a two-headed man."

I repeated, "A two-headed-man!" My eyes rolled around in my head. "How can a man have two heads?"

"Dat don't mean he got two heads. 'Dat means he got a gift, and he can tell you what's wrong wit you when the doctors don't know!"

Daddy, who called his mother by her given name said angrily, "Olivia, don't be *teachin'* Georgann to believe in that old *hoodoo mess*!"

Now, I've always believed what Mama told me, but hoodoo and the two-headed-man was something my young mind couldn't comprehend.

Aunt Clara was my least favorite great aunt. Her yellow, fat rounded humpy body, and her short pageboy hair-do worn neatly on her head, complimented her old-maidish personality. Aunt Clara's face always had a frown on it, and the word "heifer" was never far from her tobacco-spewing, smirked-up lips. Aunt Clara and her husband, Uncle Dewy, were separated. They never had any children. Aunt Clara, who worked at a café, probably didn't like children, or maybe she just didn't like me! She would order, "Gal, go emp' my spit cup!" Most times I pretended not to hear her. I felt she should have emptied her own ol' *nasty* spit cup!

"Heifer, don't you hear me?" yelled Aunt Clara. "You gon' be lazy jus' like yo' ol' Daddy!"

Being a small child, I didn't know exactly what the word heifer meant, but coming from Aunt Clara's lips, I knew it wasn't a good thing. The only times I saw Aunt Clara's frozen face cracked a smile was when the visiting preachers came to Sunday dinner and complimented her cooking.

Chapter 2
Desperate Times, Desperate Measures

Mama's good-heartedness was as big as the size of her forty-four double D bust, and she would give you her last penny. Yet, Mama was a complex person, and sometimes her perspectives of life, were confusing. My Sunday school teacher, Cousin Jessie Lee, was a light skinned, pleasingly plump lady. She had a sweet and humble personality. Her husband, David, was Mama's cousin; he was a tall, smoky black man, and an usher at church. Cousin David was as faithful at his post on Sunday nights as he was unfaithful to his wife. Being an eavesdropper on the grown-ups, they said Cousin David was like a "gyp sniffin' dog"... it didn't matter how she looked or how she smelled, as long as she had a split between her legs!

One steamy hot Sunday night, as usual, Mama and I were walking home from church. I got excited when I glanced backward and saw Cousin David's car coming our way. He and his wife never failed to stop and give Mama and me a ride home. Cousin David didn't look our way, as that old Pontiac whisked by us, flying down Hollywood Street. Mama didn't say a word.

"Mama," I asked, "who was dat woman in the car wit' Cuzzin David?"

"Hush chile!" said Mama, "Dat ain't yo' business!"

"But Mama, why would Cuzzin David have another woman in his car when he is married to Cuzzin Jessie Lee?"

Mama replied, "Now chile, you ask too many questions 'bout grown folks business."

Mama was quiet for a moment. Suddenly her footsteps came to a halt. She placed both hands on my shoulders and looked down into my eyes. "Georgann," said Mama, "I want you to remember somethin.' Don't make no difference how gooda' wife some men got, 'dey still is gonna be a man. But it's left to the woman to be the "best wife" 'dat she can be." Mama continued, "Always remember, a man can drop his *drawers* in the middle of the street and never get talked about! But let a woman do the same, and she a be the *talk* of the town!" Mama's words were engraved in my brain, and unknowingly shaped my way of thinking.

In 1952, Mama's niece moved to California and left her fully furnished home in Mama's care for an indefinite period and rent-free. The house in Mooretown was on the north side of Hollywood, on a street called Murvon. Mama had gotten a full-time job as a maid with a family in the Country Club Subdivision, within walking distance. Mama's sixteen dollars a week salary met most of our needs. She managed to buy groceries, pay our utilities, and pay fifty cents weekly to the L. B. Price salesman, who went door to door, selling goods out of the trunk of his car. When Christmas and Easter holidays came around, if her pay didn't stretch for me a new dress or pair shoes, Mama knew how to squeeze whatever she could out of *simple-minded* Aunt Ophelia. She would remind Aunt Ophelia, who worked at a motel, of her commitment to help financially. Aunt Ophelia usually came through.

***

After about two years, Mama's employer cut her days to three days a week. It produced a hardship. Aunt Ophelia wasn't able to help Mama as much because of the friction it caused between her and Uncle Zeke, Aunt Ophelia's husband. The meal barrel got low, the gas got turned off, and times were desperate. Mama decided to be a contributing factor to her philosophy … "A man is gonna be a man."

One day, when I was getting home from school, in the front yard lay an old shiny black forties Studebaker car. I ran into the house, and there was this strange man sitting at the kitchen, table eating pork chops, mashed potatoes, gravy and cornbread. He was younger than Mama, and black as tar. He had thick lips that covered his face. Mama's grin across her face was as wide as the Mississippi River. She looked at him like one looks at a priceless gem. Mama said, "Baby, this is Mister Herman, a friend of mine."

My eyes stared down at that mouth-watering pork chop on Mister Herman's plate. The only meat my eight-year-old eyes had seen lately, in our house, was that small piece of salt bacon in the Pinto Beans. I managed to get out a, "Hi, Mister Herman," without grabbing that pork chop from his plate.

Mister Herman smiled and showed the prettiest white teeth I'd ever seen. He said, "So this is Georgann. I've heard a lot 'bout you."

I wanted to say, "But I've never heard about *you*!"

Mama fixed my plate and I ate like there was no tomorrow.

Nightfall came, and Mister Herman was still visiting. I went to bed and awoke early that next morning. The first person I saw at the table was MISTER HERMAN! After that night, Mister Herman, who hauled pulpwood, became a major contributor to our household expenses. Mama no longer had to hide in the closet nor send me to the door to lie when the L. B. Price salesman came to collect. Mama was always saying, "The Lord will make a way, somehow!" Mister Herman hid in the closet on those early Saturday mornings when *Deacon Whatshisname* came to collect the weekly church dues. But, Mama and I no longer had to scrape for food. I didn't know what Mister Herman's wife and children across town were eating, but Mama and I were eating high on the hog!

Mister Herman's presence not only improved Mama's financial situation, but it produced a change in her and Daddy's volatile relationship. Working consistently wasn't in Daddy's résumé. Summer months, Daddy would caddy at the Shreveport Country Club golf course. Winter months, Daddy took a vacation. He and Mama would get into some heated arguments about his laziness. Daddy's 6ft 4in, black as midnight body extended the rollaway bed that he slept on in the kitchen. On those early cold mornings, Mama wasted the air she breathed, looking down on the blankets that covered Daddy's head. Now that Mister Herman was staying with us, I was sleeping on the rollaway bed. Disgruntled, Daddy was left with three options; sleep on a pallet on the kitchen floor, go to the Big House, or find him a woman to take care of him. Daddy did what came naturally.

Miz Gomer was her name, a woman of "independent means." She owned her home, a late model car, and had plenty of money. Miz Gomer was a petite woman whose lips had gotten parched from her habit…she was rarely seen without a beer can or whiskey bottle in her shaky hand, and a box of that lumpy Argo starch in the other. It didn't matter with

Daddy, who called all white men "Mister Charlie," that Miz Gomer was being "kept" by a Mister Charlie. Daddy had found him a meal ticket, and a risky place to stay.

It was the month of August 1955, Black magazines and newspapers across the United States carried images of the body of a fourteen-year-old colored boy named Emmett Till, who had been murdered in Mississippi. Colored folks were outraged, but some were on pins and needles.

"Lord, ham' mercy!" cried my grandmama, "How come somebod' didn't tell 'dat boy? He shoulda' known betta' than to do somethin' like 'dat!"

"Mama!" I exclaimed, "All he did was whistle at a white woman!"

Mama grabbed a hold of my arms and a shadow of fear came across her face. Her eyes looked me dead in my eyes, and she said, "Chile, you listen to me. 'Dey might do 'dat up in Chicago, Illinois where he came from, but 'dey don't do 'dat down here in the *south*!" Mama continued, "Somebod' shoulda *schooled* 'dat boy 'fore he went to Mississippi. Colored folks in the south knows 'dey place, and 'dey stays *in it*!" That awful, gruesome sight of Emmett Till's mutilated body was rooted in my memory, and put *awareness* on my ten-year-old mind. But, despite that malicious act of segregation lingering in our heads, colored people still had to carry on with their lives.

Everything was going well. Mister Herman and I had a good rapport. He was fun-loving; he took me riding in his Studebaker car, even allowed me to sit on his lap and drive. Mama's rein on me wasn't as tight. I was allowed more visits with my birth mother, who was now married, and had a whole new family. They lived across town, in the 1951-built government-owned projects, called Elamito Terrace, in an area named Lakeside/Allendale.

At Mama's reluctance, I was even allowed to spend certain weekends with Daddy and Miz Gomer. I could never stay on those first of the month weekends. Those were when Mister Charlie came to visit Miz Gomer. Mama's worst fear was that Mister Charlie was going to show up unexpectedly and catch Daddy with Miz Gomer. Her warnings were, "George, you had betta leave 'dat white man's woman alone. 'Cause if he catch you there, you can be kilt', and won't nothin' be done 'bout it!" As usual, Mama's words never fazed Daddy, except for that particular weekend. A weekend I shall never forget.

It was 1956, and segregation was as strong in Shreveport as it was in Mississippi. One particular community named Cedar Grove was downright scary.

Rumors were often floating in the air of bad incidents happening to colored people in that part of the city. Cedar Grove had its own downtown shopping center and other businesses on the main thoroughfare 70th Street. But colored people knew not to be caught on 70th Street after nightfall; it was unsafe.

On the third Friday of that month, I was to baby-sat Miz Gomer's two boys while she and Daddy went out good-timing. Just before they exited the door, the telephone rang. Suddenly Miz Gomer slammed the receiver down. Her bloodshot eyes stretched big. She spoke in a rush, "George, you gotta leave!"

"Who was that?" asked Daddy.

Miz Gomer called Mister Charlie by his name. "Old man Wilbur made a stop in Cedar Grove and is on his way here!"

Daddy's big eyes bulged. "What!"

"George!" snapped Miz Gomer, "You got to 'git yo' stuff and 'git outta' here…NOW!"

Daddy grabbed his old worn-out suitcase and began stuffing his clothes in it as fast as he could. Daddy's eyes flashed on me. "What about Georgann?" he asked. "Do you want me to take her home?"

"No." answered Miz Gomer, "She can go wit' us. I'll just tell him she's my niece."

Go wit her! I thought *where is she goin'?*

With his suitcase in his hand, Daddy's long legs hurriedly walked up the street. Daddy and Miz Gomer had a system. On the first of every month, Daddy packed his suitcase, leaves, and comes back when Mister Charlie leaves. But this time Mister Charlie broke his routine, and I was caught in the middle.

Around midnight, Miz Gomer answered the knock at her door and entered Mister Charlie, a slightly bent over, gray headed, old, and wrinkled-looking white man, wearing a plaid blue shirt, blue jeans, cowboy boots, and hat. After Miz Gomer introduced me as her niece, Mister Charlie crinkled his sunburned nose as if he smelled something fishy. He went through the house looking around suspiciously. Satisfied and looking pompous, Mister Charlie, with his pistol on his hip, gestured toward the front door, "Let's go," he said.

My chin rested on the window of Mister Charlie's 1956 black Lincoln. I inhaled the newness of the leather upholstery, giving no thought about the direction we were taking. But to get to Mister Charlie's home in Frierson, Louisiana, we had to travel on 70th Street through downtown Cedar Grove. As we were getting closer to downtown, suddenly Miz Gomer's head turned around quickly, and with her alcoholic breath, she cautioned, "When we 'git closer to town, duck y'all heads in the seat where no body can see y'all."

My insides quivered. I thought, *Oh Lordy! We gonna git hung on a tree!*

Miz Gomer, the boys, and I crunched down in the car seat. I closed my eyes tightly, afraid to open them. The car slowed down then stopped abruptly. Mister Charlie with his southern drawl, asked, "Would y'all like some hamburgers and cokes?"

Hungry, hot, and sweating, we whispered in unison, "Yes sir!"

Once we got to the outskirts of the city, on that dark and isolated road, we sat upright and enjoyed our meal. After riding, it seemed forever, we finally came upon Mister Charlie's fancy white two-story house. But my soon to be twelve-year-old eyes never got to see the inside of it. He drove about a quarter mile in back, to his unpainted shotgun house. Miz Gomer got to visit in that big fancy house twice. Her last visit was very productive and brought her a large wad of money. My eyes bucked when Miz Gomer said, "Here Georgann, this is for you," as she slipped a ten-dollar bill in my hand. That was "hush" money, for me not to tell Mama. I usually told Mama everything. But no way was I telling her *that*! Mama would have put a stop to my visits. But it wasn't long before Mama would have a more serious situation to worry about.

***

It was January, the year of 1957. One day, I rushed home from school, and in Mister Herman's place at the supper table was a vacant chair. No more Mister Herman! As suddenly as he entered our lives, he left. Mister Herman went back home to his wife and children. Mama and I were back to eating pinto beans and biscuits, and I was lying to the L. B. Price salesman. Times were hard and Mama was doing whatever measures it took to make ends meet.

One evening, around dusk, Mama said, "Come on Georgann. I want you to walk down to Miz Martha's house wit' me."

I protested, because Miz Martha didn't have any children, but Mama insisted that I come along. While Mama and Miz Martha were engrossed in conversation, I snuck off, went into our dark house, and thought, *what is this stinkin' smell?* I flicked on the light switch and there was Cousin David in *our* bed in a compromising position with *Miz So-n-So. Mama really was desperate!*

Chapter 3
Shy, Timid and Back-woods Country

As a wild flower grows, that's how I sprouted; long arms, long skinny legs, and long feet. I had my mother's brown eyes and her light-skinned tone. But I was tall, thin, and lanky, with a commanding nose like Daddy. I was constantly being reminded that I was the spitting image of "George Written." Daddy's peers would call me "Little Written." A name I preferred, rather than being called "ole-shit-color cry-baby" by a few of my darker-skinned cousins.

At twelve years old, in the sixth grade, Mama dressed me in those pretty hand-me-down dresses from two of the most expensive department stores in Shreveport; Rubenstien and Selber Brothers. *Stores poor people couldn't have afforded to buy a handkerchief from!* Mama said the Lord had blessed us through Mrs. Barsmith's kind heart. Sometimes I didn't know whether it was a blessing or a curse, especially when those dresses caused me to run for my life! After so many run-home-to-mama incidents from that *jealous* bully, Daddy cautioned Mama, "Olivia, you can't be raisin' Georgann like you help raisin' that white woman child you work for. Georgann is a colored girl, and this ain't *no* Country Club Subdivision! This is Mooretown! She had better learn to defend herself!"

That same year, while in California, Mama's niece decided she wasn't returning to Shreveport. She sold her home but gave Mama all the furniture. Mama and I moved three blocks down on that same street next door to a family whose last name was Dunbar. Mrs. Minnie Dunbar was a widow and the mother of nine; six sons and three daughters. She was about 5'4" tall, and approximately 140 pounds. Mrs. Minnie could spew out profanities quicker than Mama spit out tobacco juice. Mama said, "Minnie is a good person but she is 'bout the *cussinest* little woman I done ever seen!"

Although Mama was older than Mrs. Minnie, they became friends. Mama, who always had a sympathetic heart, understood Mrs. Minnie's plight, especially with those boys, the oldest of whom was sixteen. They were the most mischievous boys in the neighborhood. Mrs. Minnie was a Christian, but not a churchgoer, and she seemed to be overwhelmed. Her youngest son was going to be a life-long invalid and occupied most of her time.

Mama, who was big, bold, and brave, thought that she had seen it all, but she hadn't ever seen anything like Mrs. Minnie's other five boys. Mama said, "Dem boys of Minnie's is a handful. 'Dey the worse boys I've ever seen!" Sometimes Mrs. Minnie's boys would fight amongst themselves and get so out of control that she would summon Mama for help. One time, Mama returned home, shook her head, and said, "Po' Minnie, I don' know what she gonna do wit 'dem boys, 'dey don' respect nobod', not even her, 'cept for Luke, he's bout the *bestess* one of 'dem all!"

Once, Mama took me next door with her to visit Mrs. Minnie. Being an eighth grader, I had never seen anything like Mrs. Minnie's boys. One minute, they horse-played, and the next minute, a chair was thrown across the room, and one grabbed a knife and went after the other. My eyes bucked out of my head. Mama pulled me close to her, and hurriedly got me away from there.

But as frightened as I was of them, I was somewhat intrigued with their wild and rambunctious behavior and would often spy on them through my front window as they played in their yard. The one that would always capture my attention was Luke, the one Mama favored. He was a year older than me and was so cute, with a dark brown complexion, long curly eyelashes and curly hair. I had a secret crush.

There was a light breeze stirring that dusk-dark summer evening. Mama said, "Georgann, I'm gonna walk up the street to visit Cuzzin Sallybell. Do you wanna go wit' me?" she asked.

"No ma'am, Mama. I wanna stay and read my comic books."

Mama looked toward the open window and saw Luke and his brothers playing outside. "You make sho' you stay in this house. You hear me?" she warned.

"Yes ma'am."

As soon as Mama left out the front door, I ran to my favorite spot at the window, peeking. Suddenly Luke and his brothers looked my way. I jerked my head away from the window. Luke yelled out, "Georgann, I like you!" Oooh!

My heart danced around in my chest. *Luke liked me too!* After getting over that discovery, it instantly dawned on me; the water pail needed filling. I ran to the kitchen, grabbed the half-full water pail, threw the water out the back door, and made a dash outside to the front water hydrant. Watching out the corner of my eyes, Luke ran up to me. "Georgann, can I kiss you?" he asked.

The beat of my heart was pounding fast, as if it was going to explode in my chest. Then I looked up at Luke's two big front teeth and had an alarming thought. *I don't know how to kiss no boy!* But my face lit up in a shy smile, and I responded, "Yes!"

My heart pounded wildly as Luke's lips touched mine. Then... ouch! Our teeth butted. The magic moment was gone. Luke ran back to his giggling brothers. The heavy water pail seemed as light as a feather as I floated on a cloud, back into the house, all goggle-eyed and in a "puppy love" trance. Little did I know, that one-time-only awkward "teeth-butting-kiss" would help determines my destiny.

In the meantime, one of Mama's sisters, Aunt Leola, took a spell of sickness and died. Mama took Aunt Leola's job as a short-order cook at the Kick-a-Poo Café. We moved back close to Stills Quarters near the Big House in a duplex on the corner of Jewella and Mayfield Street. I didn't see Luke anymore, but Mama and Mrs. Minnie kept in touch. The only time that Mama mentioned Luke was to say that he had done something bad and had gone off to reform school.

Hearing Mama and her sisters compete with who had the best and most dramatic stories of being saved from the fiery furnace of hell by God never got dull. During those hot summer months, the family would form a circle on late evenings under that old weeping willow tree, fanning flies and swatting at mosquitoes. Mama Puddin' always had a smile planted on her face. Nannie puffed on a cigarette, and the remaining sisters spewed out tobacco juice and snuff spit to the ground.

Although I heard them tell their stories over and over, as a young child, they never failed to captivate me. I would become frightened out of my wits by their eloquent tales, complete with gestures and their vivid expressions that were artistically painted and etched in my imagination. My eyes would widen, and I would grab at my heart, fascinated as one after the other gave their testimonies. They all had their own unique stories, even old "sourpuss" Aunt Clara.

It was the summer of 1958, and revival time. Two weeks of toes tapping, hands clapping, hymns singing and preaching good times. Those once-a-year summer revival events in July were highly anticipated. Soon I was to become fourteen years old, and I was still on what was called the "mourners bench." Two consecutive summer revivals I had given God my heart and the Preacher my hand, but never followed through with the baptism. But that summer, I was baptized and I finally became an official member of Morning Star Baptist Church.

That same year, Daddy and Miz Gomer's relationship came to an end. I guess Daddy got tired of Miz Gomer's drunkenness and Miz Gomer got tired of Daddy's freeloading ways. Now Daddy was a permanent live-in with Mama and me, until they fell out with each other; then Daddy would seek shelter at the Big House. At this point, Daddy was working regularly and Mama was getting financial assistance from him…some times.

Early that Friday morning, Daddy was in the kitchen, frying bacon, scrambling eggs, and whistling along with his favorite Bobby Blue Bland blues on the colored KOKA radio station. Today was payday! Daddy had diligently gotten up early all week and gone to work, caddying at the Country Club. Before he walked out the door, Mama reminded him, "George, don't forget 'dat you promised to pay six dollars to the rent man in the mornin'."

Daddy looked annoyed. "Olivia, you don't have to remind me. I know Mister Charlie is gonna show up early tomorrow morning."

"Yeah George, but I know *you*!" said Mama. "So, when you git off work, you bring 'dat money to Georgann so she can keep it."

Friday evening, I waited and waited. Around seven o'clock I walked up Jewella to Hollywood Avenue. It wasn't my first time going on a search for Daddy. There were three juke joints on Hollywood Avenue that Daddy frequented; one was called Paradise Bar, on the west end of Hollywood. In the middle was the Blue Note Inn, and the one that was closest to Jewella was called Hollywood Bar. Some Friday and Saturday nights, between the seven and eight o'clock hours, I had made all three bars… trying to make sure I found Daddy before he *wasted* his money.

At the red light, I crossed Hollywood Avenue in a hurry. I was desperate to get to that white framed, bright, neon lit building. I thought, *I'm gonna make sho' Daddy gives Mama some money this time!* My being fourteen years old didn't allow me to enter the building. As the door swung back and forth with people coming and going, I was undaunted by the curious stares as I stood on the outside of Hollywood Bar, hoping Daddy would come outside. Finally, I spotted a man who knew Daddy. "Mr. Walpoo!" I called out, "if you see my daddy in there, will you tell him his daughter is outside wantin' to see him?"

"Okay Little Written," he replied.

With great expectancy, I stood waiting patiently by those steps counting patrons, smelling beer, whiskey, and wine. I could hear those loud voices of laughter and those "honky-tonking" down home blues. Finally, the door opened, and Mr. Walpoo looked down on me and said, "Little Written, he ain't in here."

My heart sunk. I thought, *Now, what is Mama gonna do?*

Mama got home from work about twelve-thirty that night, weary looking and holding her back.

"Mama," I said, "Daddy didn't come home, and I couldn't find him."

Mama sighed and shook her head in disappointment.

Saturday afternoon, around 1:30 p.m., Mama grimaced in pain as she rose up in bed. "Come here Georgann and rub this liniment on my back."

The stench of Watkins liniment could be smelled throughout our small duplex. Its strength was so intense, it had my hands burning as I applied it to mama's back.

"Mama," I said, "how you gonna go to work today? You hardly can walk."

"Baby, I gotta go to work. We need the money. The 'lectric gonna git cut off."

"But, how come you won't *make* Daddy help you? Ain't nothin' wrong wit' him. He can *help* you!"

"Chile, now you know I caint depend on 'dat daddy of yo's! He might bring some money home and he might not. So, I had betta git to work so these bills can be paid."

The liniment didn't work its magical cure. Mama's face was frowned-up from pain and worrying. "I don't know what I'm gonna do 'bout the 'lectric bill," said Mama. "Lord! I need a blessin'!"

Suddenly Mama and I heard a familiar voice whistling from afar. I went to the door and there was Daddy walking up Jewella whistling his favorite song, *I Don't Want No Woman Tellin' Me What to Do.*

I stood in the door, watching Daddy walk. His right shoulder was elevated high, and he had a stroll as if he owned the universe. Resentment boiled over in me. I thought, *How can Daddy be in such a jolly mood after makin' a promise to Mama about payin' the rent and he didn't even come home? Now here he comes showin' up the next day!* Angrily, I said under my breath, "He just makes me sick! I betcha he ain't got two nickels to rub together. Half the time he doesn't work, and when he does work he don't wanna give his Mama any money! Mama oughta just put'im out!" I thought, *one thang I know, when I get grown I'm sho' not marryin' a man like him. With his ole triflin' self!*

Daddy came through the door sniffing up his nose. "Olivia's back must be botherin' her again?"

I rolled my eyes at the back of Daddy's head. "Yeah Daddy," I said, "Mama ain't able to go to work this evening. And she is worried about the electric bill gettin' paid, 'cause she used the electric bill money to pay the rent."

Daddy's big eyes got a glint in them and a smile crossed his face. He stood over Mama's bed, went into his pants pocket and came out with a wad of dollar bills. He threw the money on the bed like he was throwing dice. "Here Olivia," said Daddy, "is that enough?"

Mama and I were flabbergasted. Her eyes bulged, "I was jus' askin' God for a blessin' and here you come wit this money." Mama's face tightened and her eyes narrowed, "Boy, where you git all this money from?" she asked.

Daddy looked into my grinning face and winked, "I got it on my knees, but I wasn't prayin'!" said Daddy.

Mama frowned, "Alright George, you start makin' fun and God gon' *git* you!"

"Olivia, don't worry 'bout where I got it from. You asked God for a blessin'... now accept yo' blessin'!"

My feelings for Daddy could sometimes be conflicting. I loved him most times and couldn't *stand* him other times. I didn't understand how he could see the struggles his mother was having, raising me, his daughter, (and in good conscience) not do all he could to help her. I would get angry with Mama for allowing Daddy to take advantage of her generosity; if he didn't work, she fed him. While she got out on those cold mornings, going to work, Daddy stayed in bed. In the mid-afternoon, Daddy finally got up, dressed in his nice clean slacks and shirt, puts on his Old Spice after shave, and strolls up Jewella, gallivanting around Mooretown, dodging work. When Mama would get fed up, there would be an altercation, and she would put Daddy out. As always, he sought shelter at the big house. Mama felt sorry for him, and allows him back in, time and time again. Sometimes I wanted to light a *fire* under *Daddy's butt*!

On the other hand, Daddy could be very charming, and he had the cooking skills of a chef. One time he cooked my favorite meal of pork steak smothered in tomato paste gravy, with rice and cornbread; that made my mouth water. My hands couldn't feed my face fast enough. Daddy said, "Slow down Kiddo, the food ain't gone run off!"

I thought, *yeah, the food ain't gone run off. But, after a while you gone take off, and not work. So, I had better eat good, while the eatin' **is** good!*

***

In the month of June, 1959, I felt that I had come of age. No longer should I wear those homemade dresses that I had worn in junior high, and my pencil legs needed *stockings*. Around eleven o'clock that Saturday morning the trolley stopped on downtown Texas Avenue, and all you could see were people; high-yellow, light-brown, medium brown, black, smut black, shiny black and ashy black...Colored people from near and far. Oh yes! And shit-color, too! Texas Avenue was the main street for poor folks to shop, and businesses flourished from money earned by those hard-working hands of cotton pickers, ditch-diggers, maids, and others. Shucks, Colored folks should have owned *shares of stock* from those department stores on downtown Texas!

Mama had given me five dollars; two dollars for trolley fare and treats, and three dollars for my lay-a-way. Off I went to Grayson Department store, where I put on layaway; four outfits, undergarments and stockings. Afterward, I headed down to the Woolworth Discount store and waited at the crowded "colored section" lunch counter to chow down on one of their greasy chili-dogs.

It was the beginning of a new era. I was entering my sophomore year and going to a school that I had heard so much about, Booker T. Washington, the only public high school in the Shreveport area for Blacks. That summer, I was excited with anticipation.

I couldn't recall ever hearing Daddy mentioning his last school grade completed. However, I did notice he had very nice penmanship. So, the last week of my summer vacation, around six thirty on that hot summer Saturday evening, Daddy and I were walking up the old black top Jewella road, headed for the Big House. As my legs tried to keep up with Daddy's long legs walking in a hasty pace, he said, "Come on,

Kiddo, it's just about seven o'clock! And I don't want to miss the beginning of *Gunsmoke*."

I ran up beside Daddy.

"Kiddo, you'll be going to high school next week, right?"

A smile covered my face.

"Yep, and I can't wait! Bonse I'll be in the tenth grade!"

Suddenly, Daddy's legs came to a halt. He looked down at me with a frown on his face. "Georgann, don't you go to that school using *that* word!"

"What word, Daddy?"

"Bonse!" said Daddy. "And all those other old slavish words that you heard yo' grandmama Olivia using." Daddy paused, then started making snapping sounds with two of his fingers, and saying, "Ah, ah...oh yea! "sumpin' teet" (something to eat). That old country word Mama Puddin' and all the rest of the old folks in this family use." Daddy continued, "I'm tellin' you now, if you go to that high school using them words, those kids are going to make fun of you!"

As we resumed walking, I turned my head and turned my nose up. I thought to myself, *Daddy gets on my nerve! He is always tryin' to correct me and tell me how to talk. But can't nobody tell him how he needs to keep a job! If he would work and help his*

Mama more, we wouldn't be havin' to go to the Big House to watch television. We should have our own!

The Lakeside\Allendale area was a long way from Mooretown. It was in the northeast part of the city, and closer to downtown. And as one of the city's oldest sections, it was considered to be a cut above any of the other Black areas, especially Mooretown. Lakeside/Allendale was where the "who's who" lived; the Black lawyers, doctors, dentists, and majority of the teachers ...the sophisticated people. It was the community which housed the greatest number of enterprising Black business owners. And in the center of it all, on a street named Milam, was the preeminent Booker T. Washington High School.

That September day, I had on my new outfit and my seamed Red Fox stockings on my pencil legs. I stepped on the campus of Booker T. Washington and was intimidated by its size. That two-story building was bigger than life and overwhelming. Students from all areas of the city were there, but the Lakeside/Allendale students could easily be identified... They walked around campus with an air of superiority about themselves...or so I thought. My insecurities stuck out like a cactus growing among daisies.

Mrs. Sartor's class was where I belonged... learning how to beautify the hair. I wanted to become a beautician. Sometimes I became my own "jack leg" beautician, working on my hair and other family members that were brave enough to allow me to practice my skills. In Mrs. Sartor's classroom were sophomore, junior, and senior girls. One Friday we had to work on each other's hair. An uppity Lakeside gal pointed to me. "I'm going to do her hair," said "Miss Sidity."

My eyes bucked. I thought, *Oh Lordy! She gonna burn my scalp!*

Quickly I spoke, "Ah, that's alright, 'cause mine don't need doing, bonse I just did it last night."

She rolled her eyes and tossed her shoulders, "*Bonse!*" she giggled. "Where you get *that* country word from?"

All eyes were on me. I wished the floor had opened up and swallowed me.

My soft toned voice whined, "My grandmama says *bonse* all the time!"

"There's no such word!" she snapped. "So, don't be bringin' that old *country word* up in here!"

I felt insecure, immature, and back-woods country. Imagine if I had used the word, "sumpin' teet!" They would have laughed me out of the classroom.

My grandmama made a scaredy-cat out of me, and my behavior was conditioned by my fears. When I became thirteen and the pains from those monthly cramps caused me to stay in bed, Mama said, "Chile, these pains ain't *nothin'* compared to childbirth. Some people die havin' a baby." Then she would tell me about the "death angel" visiting a woman in labor. Mama said that a woman in labor is close to death at least twice, but if the death angel visits her that third time, she'll die from childbirth. Mama had frightened me with that story, so much so, I never wanted to have a baby. Her other controlling method was, "Georgann, I might not see everythang you do, but God sees it. And He will punish you!" Mama put the fear of God in my heart, and I was afraid to do anything contrary to my upbringing. If so, something was going to fall out of the sky and hit me in the top of my head!

***

It was May of 1960, and school was out. I was a restless fifteen-year-old. My attitude and personality were noticeably changing. I was at that age: rude, sullen, and hard to live with. And behind Mama's back, I had the nerve to roll my eyes at her. Suddenly, having to go to church on Sundays, choir practice on Tuesdays, and reading my Modern Romance and True Story magazines became boring. I needed some excitement for the summer. And who was better to supply me with some summer excitement? None other than a girl named Tootie.

My cousin, Tootie, was as bold and fast as I was scared and slow. Tootie was on the heavy side, very busty with a pretty face and too worldly for her age. She had always poked fun at me, saying with a snicker, "Georgann, you're such a square! What do you do for fun?"

"I like to dance."

Tootie looked at me with a smirk on her face saying, "Come spend the night wit' me, and we'll go to the juke joint and dance." She dared me.

"Oooh Girl! I can't go to *no* juke joint. I'm scared Daddy might catch me in there!"

But that one particular Friday morning, I got up bright and early; within the hour Mama woke up to grits, bacon, and sliced toast. Mama sat down at the table with a pleased smile. "Georgann, dat's mighty nice of you to fix my breakfast without bein' told."

"Yes ma'am." I hesitated, "Mama, I have somethin' to ask you."

"Well, what is it?"

"Tootie want me to stay all night with her. Will it be alright wit' you?"

Mama placed her chin in her hand and sighed long and heavy. Finally, she gave me a long, hard look in my eyes. "Georgann, I'm gonna let you stay the night wit' dat *fast-tail* gal. But I betta not hear of you doin' somethin' you ain't s'posed to be doin'. You hear?"

"Yes ma'am, I hear you."

"Cause its one thang for sho', I might not see everythang you do, but *God* sees it!""Mama, I ain't gonna do nothin' bad."

On that hot summer Friday in July, about dusk, Tootie and I walked the streets of Mooretown, headed to Paradise Bar on the west end of Hollywood Avenue. I felt for the first time daring and adventurous. I couldn't wait to get my feet on that dance floor. Mama had seen me "cut a rug," as she put it, and would always comment, "Chile, you can jitterbug jus' like yo' Daddy!" But I had always held back on some of my dance moves, thinking that Mama wouldn't approve. I thought, *When I get on that juke joint floor, I'm gonna let it all hang out!*

The closer we got to Paradise Bar, the more nervous and excited I became. At the steps I lost my nerve. "Tootie," I said, "go inside first and see if my daddy is in there. And see if there's anybody we think knows us."

"Alright," said Tootie, "wit yo' scary self!"

Tootie could have cared less who knew her.

I hid around the corner of the building, peeking.

Within a moment, the door opened and Tootie beckoned for me. She said in a whisper, "The coast is clear!"

The room was slightly dark, with red and blue lights illuminating the dance floor. With her lips painted heavily in bright red lipstick, and a cigarette dangling from her sixteen-year-old lips, Tootie walked over to the bar. The bartender asked, "What you havin'?"

"I'll have a Tom Collins," said Tootie.

I went to the jukebox and put a nickel in it, selecting the latest hit song with a fast beat. I began to dance. My long string bean legs were twisting and twirling, dancing with wild abandonment, as if it was the last dance I would ever do. I didn't miss a beat of that music. After the music stopped, I suddenly came down to reality and thought, *What if my daddy caught me in this place?* I said to Tootie, "Let's get outta here!"

As we started crossing to the other side of the street, I looked west to see if there was any traffic approaching…all clear. Then I looked east and saw a sight that was both frightening and mesmerizing. There, in the middle of Hollywood Avenue, appeared to be a big round glowing orange ball that spread over both sides of the street. In the middle of this sight appeared to be an image, with two big piercing eyes.

I yelled out, "Tootie! Tootie! Look, there's Jesus and He is staring at us!" Tootie looked up, she and I both screamed simultaneously. I shouted out, "Oh Lord! I'm so sorry! Please forgive me!"

Tootie threw her paper-cup of alcohol to the ground, threw-up both her hands in the air, yelling, "Please Lord! Give me another chance!" as we began running. Tootie and I were picking our feet up and putting them down as fast as they would go. After a few strides, I sprinted away from Tootie. My long skinny legs were galloping, making long strides onto the ground. As I glanced back, a cloud of dust was between Tootie and me. Her big tree trunk legs could not keep pace with mine.

Tootie yelled, "Georgann! Georgann! Wait for me!"

I thought, *Shoot! Tootie must be crazy if she thinks I'm slowin' down. Jesus is after me, and I am runnin' for cover.* Within the next block, my stride began slowing down, because the closer I got, the smaller the image seemed to have gotten. The big ball seemingly was getting smaller, the image fading away, ascending into the sky.

Suddenly, Tootie was beside me, and we came to a standstill. Our eyes widened, and our head and neck stuck out as we gawked at the sight. Tootie and I looked at each other and burst into hysterical laughter.

We realized it had only been the reflection of the sunset.

That one, frightful night experience was enough excitement for me that summer and put an end to my teenage "honky tonking" days. That following Sunday morning, I was glad to be in Sunday school class listening to my sweet humble teacher, Sister Jessie Lee, instructing us about Christian behavior. I wanted to witness, "Amen! Amen!"

My temporary relationship with Tootie came to an abrupt end. I developed a more stable and lasting friendship with two sisters named Mary and Earnestine Terrell, who also were my cousins. We had more in common; we sang in the church choir and had weekend sleepovers. Sometimes we would listen to the boogie-woogie music on the radio, and dance until our legs were weak. I was having the time of my life. However, my lazy, nonchalant, carefree life was about to come to an end.

Chapter 4
Awakening of My Conscience

"D'Artois don't play!" that was rumored in the colored community. George W. D'Artois, a long-nosed, crew cut-wearing former Marine Corps Sergeant who grew up in Shreveport, was now a Captain in the Caddo Sheriff's Department.

Daddy said, "That redneck peckerwood D'Artois, might as well wear a sign 'round his neck that reads...NIGGERS AND FLIES, I DO DESPISE!"

"Hush, George!" said Mama, "Don't be talkin' dat kinda talk in front of this chile, jus' cause you don't like *white folks*."

"Georgann got to learn about the *facts of life!*" said Daddy. "You can't keep this girl from growing-up. Georgann is fifteen years old, and you still want her to call the devil... *Badman!*"

Daddy really had gotten under Mama's skin. Her nose flared. She bristled to the kitchen and grabbed the one pound package of Pinto Beans off the shelf. Mama gave her son a cold stare, and snapped, "You got two-bits, so we can have some *fatback* to cook wit' these beans?"

Looking sheepish, Daddy shook his head, "Naw, Olivia."

"Um hmm, jus' as I thought," said Mama. "Well, go up to Cangelose store and tell Henry I said let you git twenty-five cent worth a Dry Salt Bacon."

"Now Olivia, you know I'm not going up to that store, *beggin'* them Dagos!"

"Boy!" cried Mama, *"shame on you!"* She folded her arms under her large breasts, shook her head and said, "Georgann, baby, gon' up to the store, git' the dry salt, and ask Mister Henry will he put it on my account 'til Friday, and a plug of Day's Work Tobacco, too." Mama unfolded her arms, and her breasts flopped to her fat protruding stomach that had held many *on credit meals*. She spoke up, "Henry is a *good* man. He treats colored folks fair by allowin' credit 'til payday. 'Cause some of us ain't got much mo' than God gave a snake ... dat's grass to crawl in!" Mama shook her finger at Daddy and said, "Now, Son... *dat's a fact of life!*"

***

It was the month of August 1960. Daddy wasn't working and didn't show any interest in finding work. His excuses were that the younger caddies were taking over at the Country Club, and nobody else was hiring. Daddy's and Mama's relationship was at odds again, so he retreated to the Big House. Mama became an *Entrepreneur*!

Every Saturday around noon, like clock work, those same three faithful men customers were welcomed to Mama's bedroom with empty hands and left with something in a brown paper bag. Those Saturday noon visitors began to appear at odd hours late at night. That Friday night, while Mama was at work, my snooping eyes were like a hawk as I rambled in Mama's bedroom; poking my hands in drawers, behind that makeshift closet, under her bed and lastly between her mattress. *I found it!*

Saturday morning couldn't come quickly enough. Mama had barely put one foot on the floor when I was up in her face, holding the evidence in my hand. I felt somewhat smug; I was the parent and she was the child. A kind of righteous indignation rose up in me.

"Mama" I snapped, "Why is liquor being kept under yo' mattress?"

Mama's eyes widened, "I'm sorry you found 'dat. I tried to hide it from you."

"Why are you doin' this, when you're always tryin' to teach me right from wrong?"

"Georgann, I know 'dat it's wrong, but I need the extra money to make ends meet. Wit' you in high school and needin' extra thangs, I don't make a nuff money to git'em!"

Her answer wiped that smug look from my face. I suddenly saw a fifty-eight-year old woman, who had worked hard all her life, with an income of only $27 weekly. She was struggling hard to make it, doing the best she could do for me. Last school season, I talked her into allowing me to ride the public transportation to school instead of the free school bus. I had to have store-bought clothes and stockings instead of socks. These were things that we couldn't afford. She went without her needs, putting safety pins in her worn-out panties and cardboard in her shoes. This was a turning point for me, a defining moment.

"Mama, let me get a baby sittin' job so I can help you," I pleaded.

"No, chile, you jus' go to school so you can git'a education."

"But Mama, you can get caught and go to jail."

"Don't you worry 'bout this 'cause I ain't gonna go to no *jail*," she reassured me. "I'll stop when you finish high school."

The length and depth of Mama's love and sacrifice went beyond boundaries. Now, when Mama came home after working the night shift at the Kick-a-Poo Café, her brassiere held more than her *breasts*! And her long lined high waist girdle was holding in place more than her *bad back*! My conscience was awakened. I no longer hid in the outhouse, hoping wiggling yellow maggots didn't crawl up my *sorry* butt, pretending to have stomachaches so Mama would do the dirty dishes. Those chores that Mama had scolded me about became an automatic task. In retrospect, I felt responsible for Mama's bootlegging business. I could picture those white policemen, who were known to put their billy clubs to Colored folks' heads, and their ol' snitcher colored policeman, Leemon Brown (who Colored folks said would snitch on his *own* Mother), beating my grandmama and taking her off to jail. Hearing those late-night knocks at the door ... I was scared *shitless*!

***

The first back-to-school day of that September, I awoke at 5 a.m., lying quietly on my back, trying to decide which new outfit I was going to wear to school. Then, I heard Mama's voice in a whisper, *"Lord, take care of my chile. Throw Yo' arms of protection 'round her. Keep her safe from all hurt, harm and danger...and Lord, not only her, but all the chilluns!"* Mama's whispering voice had urgency in it, and rightly so. Black folks were staging sit-ins and boycotts for equality throughout the city, and they were being put in jail, faster than a rat nibbled on cheese.

Mama paced the floor and wringed her hands nervously. "Georgann!" said Mama. Now don't you go up to dat school tryin' to protest. I'm sendin' you to school to learn and git'a education!" She continued, "I ain't got no money to be gittin' you outta jail. And dat ol' low-down D'Artois and his posse would jus' as soon arrest you as look at ya'! You hear?"

"Yes, ma'am Mama! I hear you!" I thought, *Mama, you don't have to tell me about no protestin'. The idea of D'Artois's posse puttin' their clubs up side of my head scares the life out of me!*

Civil unrest in Shreveport was on the rise, and D'Artois, who was notorious for knowing how to keep the Black folks in line, was tearing through the Black community.

Lakeside/Allendale was the "hot bed" gathering for meetings of the Civil Rights Movement.

Some black folks were risking their lives and being hauled off to jail in paddy wagons for protesting for the betterment of Black people. A brazen young preacher named Harry Blake was becoming just as well-known in Shreveport in his fight for equality of Blacks as George D'Artois was for using billy clubs upside the heads of Blacks. Some older Blacks' fear of D'Artois derailed their thinking. They didn't know whether to "shit or get off the pot!" They thought Reverend Harry Blake, who came right off the plantation of Dixie, Louisiana, by way of Bishop College in Dallas, Texas, had the nerves of a "brass ass monkey!"

The rivaling young Black gang members, fighting over neighborhood turf, seemed to have no fear of

D'Artois. They fought wherever and whenever they could. Football games at the stadium were a common place for fights, as well as the school campus.

So far my junior year at Booker T. Washington was going smoothly. I learned that those Lakeside/Allendale girls weren't as snotty as I had first thought. In mid-October, 1960, the weather was sunny and mild. Students were sitting lazily on the campus lawn during lunch period, waiting for the bell to ring, when suddenly out of nowhere, a fight broke out; three non-students attacked a student. They viciously and brutally stomped and kicked the student as he cowered in a fetal position. It was the most vicious act of violence I'd ever seen. The non-students were outfitted with blue overalls, one strap fastened and the other strap hanging from their back. I recognized them immediately, and the one that was most recognizable was of all people, Luke Dunbar!

Luke looked out in the crowd and his eyes connected with mine. Suddenly he looked ashamed; his eyes shifted away. Their little gang then dispersed, running from the school grounds. Luke's gang activity made me sick to my stomach and left no doubt in my mind what Luke was…a hoodlum. But, maybe he could change his behavior with the right influence. I had not forgotten that warm summer night under the stars, hearing the pounding of my heart as I experienced my first kiss.

I never mentioned that schoolyard incident to Mama. However, Luke's involvement in gang activities caused his notorious reputation to spread rampantly throughout our community. Mama, along with the rest of the family members, had a very low opinion of Luke.

***

December 5, 1960. For my sixteenth birthday present, Mama's *bootlegging* money bought our very first television set; a black and white, floor model Zenith. Not only that, we were having a big juicy T-bone steak smothered in gravy for Sunday dinners, on occasions. Life was good. I sailed through my junior year with great anticipation. It would be my last year attending Booker T. Washington.

The buzz surrounding the Mooretown area that summer was the big news about our new school and who was going to be its principal. Everybody was excited. A brand-new school would bring life into our dead community. Not only were the citizens of Mooretown getting a new school, but the area was also getting a face-lift, being revitalized with new modern homes in the heart of the community. Old existing homes were also being revitalized with one of the best inventions that God allowed; indoor plumbing. No more slop-jars and outhouses!

The grown-ups were also excited about the new school, but some were apprehensive about its new principal, Mr. Albert Moody. It was rumored that Mr. Moody was regarded highly among his peers. The rumor also claimed that Mr. Moody was a dignified man, with a kind heart and gentle spirit, and everyone that knew him, loved him. But he probably wouldn't know how to handle Mooretown's children. Daddy was one of those skeptical persons.

The lawn at the Big House was the place I liked to be on Sunday evenings. That old weeping willow tree made good shade for those gatherings as family members and friends dropped by for visits, talking about any and everything. On this particular Sunday, Deacon John, our community activist, who was no stranger to the Big House, was among those gathered. Daddy, took a long puff from his cigarette, exhaled the smoke, making a circle in the air. He looked over at Deacon John and asked, "John, what do you know about the principal that the new school is gettin'?"

"I dunno," said Deacon John, "but I heard he's a good man. And that he was gonna give all school-aged children that had dropped out of school a second chance to get an education."

Daddy's eyes lit up, "Yeah?"

"Yep!" said Deacon John. "They say Mr. Moody is gonna find out what grade that child stopped in, and is gonna put him or her back in that grade, so they can have an opportunity like any other child."

Daddy flipped his cigarette to the ground and squashed it out with his foot. "You mean to tell me that even them ol' young thugs that always fightin' and giving Mooretown a bad name will be allowed to go back to school too?" questioned Daddy.

Deacon John shrugged his shoulders and said, "I guess so. The way I hear it, Mr. Moody has a lot of patience with children. And he is willin' to give any child a chance. As long as they come to school and abide by the rules."

"Well, I'll tell you one thing," said Daddy. "I hope he will have a big stick to go along with them rules! 'Cause if he let them Mooretown thugs come there, he gonna need a baseball bat to put upside *their* heads!"

Our new school, Bethune, was located at the corner of Henry Street and Kennedy Drive. It was on the north side of Hollywood Avenue. The school was directly across from a cemetery called, Zion Rest. And the school was surrounded by more modern homes than the south side of Mooretown.

In September 1961, my senior year, I began the long walk to our brand new school, Bethune Junior and Senior High. That first day of school the office was cluttered with school drop-outs. The children seemed to come out the woodwork! And in the midst of it all was Mr. Moody. He was as black as midnight. He stood tall and straight, and his body moved with swiftness. My first impression of our principal was that he was a man of great character. I could feel his caring spirit, it showed through his communication with the students. The most kind and gentle principal I had ever encountered...we all fell in love with Mr. Moody.

Excitement filled the air! The beautiful new school building, new desks and chairs, even new books! The building was large enough to accommodate the students, yet small enough to feel comfortable, surrounded by those familiar faces I had known from elementary school. This was going to be the best year of my school life.

By the third week of school, while sitting in the cafeteria eating my lunch, I glanced up... my heart skipped a beat. He was an inch shy of six feet, with broad shoulders, narrow waistline, chocolate complexion, dark brown eyes lined with long black lashes - strong and tender all wrapped up in one package. We stared at each other. My heart began beating erratically, and my senses took a leave of absence. I thought, *Oh my God! Of all the boys in school, why is my heart pounding with excitement over this boy?*

At the end of the school day, I went to my locker to gather all my books and my heart started fluttering. There he was, waiting for me.

"Georgann, can I take yo' books and walk you home?" he asked.

"Sure," I responded, trying to be "cool" while my heart pounded excessively. I was afraid it could be seen through my blouse.

As we strolled lazily along the street, I felt a brand-new world about to open up.

"Do you have a boyfriend?" he asked.

"No, I don't," I replied.

"Would it be alright if I came to see you?"

"Yes, you can come to see me."

We arrived at my house too soon. I didn't want him to go.

His eyes were staring into mine with so much tenderness. He held my hand and said, "I'll see you tomorrow." At that moment I knew there would never be another boy for me.

That night I fantasized about being held in his arms. I tossed and turned most of the night. I reached over and hugged the pillow, pulling it close to my body and snuggling up to it, enjoying the warm sensation of being held. *Wow! What a night.*

The next morning, I could barely contain my enthusiasm. I arrived at school earlier than ever to congregate in the courtyard. Somehow, I knew he would be there. I saw him standing at the edge of the crowd. Our eyes met. I felt like I was floating on a cloud. This was certainly no schoolgirl crush, and he was no ordinary boy. However, I was in a dilemma. How was I going to get Mama's permission for him to come courting?

Saturday morning at the breakfast table, Mama was in a high-spirited mood as she said grace. As we sat across from each other inhaling the delicious aroma of cured sliced ham and anticipating those hot buttered biscuits, I gave Mama one of my sweetest smiles.

"Mama," I said. "I have somethin' to ask you."

"What is it, Georgann?"

"Would it be alright if Luke comes to see me?"

Mama bit into her biscuit hungrily. "Luke!" said Mama, "Luke who?"

"You know. Luke Dunbar, Mrs. Minnie's son."

Mama's eyes stretched bigger than that biscuit she choked on. She coughed and sputtered, flailing her arms, gasping for breath.

"Mama! Mama! Are you alright?" My hand frantically patted her back.

Nodding, and clearing her throat, she stared at me as if I was crazy, and screamed-out, "HELL NAW! NOT 'DAT GANGSTA'!"

"Mama, Luke has changed. He ain't in a gang anymore. He's in school gettin' an education."

"I don't care what you say. Dat boy ain't the type of boy for you. He's jus' no good!" she yelled.

"But Mama, you said that Luke was the *best one* of the Dunbar boys."

"Yes, I said 'dat 'cause 'dey all is bad! But he seems to show more respect than 'dem others. Still, 'dat don't mean he can court you."

"Mama, I'm old enough to pick my own boyfriend. When are you gonna stop tryin' to tell me who to like?"

She was astounded.

I realized I had put my foot in my mouth.

Mama sprang up out of her chair. Her right hand drew back to slap my face.

I froze in shock.

Mama caught herself. She sighed heavily, "Georgann, I'm jus' lookin' out for yo' best interest," she said. "I tried to bring you up right, and 'dat boy ain't right for you. He caint come to court you, and I *meant* it!"

In the past, I usually would get my way with Mama, but all of my pleading, begging and pouting was in vain. Mama was adamant that I was not to have anything to do with Luke Dunbar. Angrily, I thought,

Mama can't tell me who to like. I'm old enough to make my own decision!

I defied Mama.

After school, Luke continued to walk with me the distance about a half block from my house. My heart did flip-flops from him holding my hand. And my skinny legs became weak and wobbly just being in his presence. I was overwhelmed by love! But Luke abruptly quit school the latter part of November.

***

Mama and my daddy had never been in agreement about how she was raising me. Now they seemed to have formed an alliance. Daddy's inconsistent work habits and his weekend's "bar hopping" became irrelevant. Now on Friday and Saturday nights, for the most part, his sized 14's were propped-up in front of the TV that Mama was making those monthly payments on, imitating a regular stay-at-home, wanna-be dad.

One Saturday morning at the breakfast table, Daddy looking under his eyes at me, as if he held his tongue any longer it would become glued to his mouth, said, "Kiddo, I heard about what happened the other day to that nice principal at y'all school."

My face frowned. "What happened?"

Daddy's head came up and he stared me in the eyes. He spoke sharply, "Girl, don't you know anything? That bunch of Mooretown hoodlums caused Mr. Moody to hurt himself the other day!"

"Who told you that, Daddy?"

"Everybody is talkin' about it!" said Daddy. "They say the gang that Luke be with came on the school campus and tried to jump on a boy there. Mr. Moody fell and hurt himself tryin' to run them off the campus."

"But Daddy, Luke don't go to school anymore! He got a job."

"Yes, he got a job. One reason why, is because he's not allowed on the school campus anymore."

I looked at my daddy's neat, self-manicured nails and hands that showed no evidence of hard work, and I wanted to say, "At least Luke has a job!" But no matter what I sometimes thought about my daddy, I knew not let my mouth overload my ass!

Luke got a job with a construction company working in our neighborhood. Now I couldn't wait for the school day to end, so that I could see Luke on those streets of Mooretown. His body was wet with sweat and his blue overalls covered with dirt from digging those ditches, laying plumbing pipes - *making a productive contribution to the Mooretown area!* Luke's appearance never diminished my love. If anything, it brought my attention to the fact that he wasn't lazy. And that fact was highly impressive; *Luke had a J-O-B!!*

Chapter 5
Real-Life Drama

During this period of time, Captain D'Artois's political career was on the rise. With his notoriety as having been a "kick-ass" jungle fighter in the Marine Corps, he resigned from being a captain, to run for Shreveport's highest job in law-enforcement; Commissioner of Public Safety. With his experience, he was going to keep the city of Shreveport safe for white folks; Black folks...FEAR!

The peaking Civil Rights Movement had caused the brazen young preacher Reverend Harry Blake to receive threats on his life and bullets to his car.

"Lord! Jesus!" cried Mama, "Dat boy is gonna fool 'round and git hisself kilt'!"

Many Blacks were jeopardizing their lives, being locked up for the cause, fighting for our rights. Shame on me, protesting and demonstrating wasn't in my DNA! It passed over my head like a cloud. Stuck in my own little fantasy world, the only rights my scared monkey ass was fighting for were the right to have my lips locking up with Luke's lips!

***

Saturday morning, December 5, 1961, I awoke with excitement. *Today is my birthday. I am seventeen years old, and I am old enough to make my own decisions.* Mama and I were not exactly on friendly terms, but Mama was not going to let an important occasion like this go unacknowledged. She presented me with a surprise birthday present, a phonograph player. I rushed to her and threw my arms around her big soft cushioning body. "Ooh, thank you Mama! Thank you!" In the midst of my rebelliousness, I had not lost sight of the fact that Mama made many sacrifices for my sake. However, Mama's sacrifices were not going to interfere with what was on my agenda.

Three o'clock p.m., Mama walked up to the corner of Jewella and Hollywood to the bus stop, for work. I had four hours to prepare. I read my True Story and Modern Romance magazines and listened on the new phonograph player to my favorite Jerry Butler song, "For Your Precious Love." By 6:55 pm, I was already lost in my fantasy world.

At seven o'clock, Luke arrived with a beautifully wrapped box. "I bought you somethin' for yo' birthday," he said.

"What is it?" I asked.

"Open it," he said. "I hope you like it."

Carefully unwrapping the present as not to tear the paper, I wondered what could be in this large box. My heart was pounding with excitement, I held my breath.

A raincoat—a pink floral raincoat with a matching rain hat!

"Oh, Luke, this is so pretty and somethin' I really need."

Luke took me in his arms, and I was "ripe for the picken." Luke's hands were exploring my body, touching me in places that no teenage girl should be touched. My body was experiencing a sensation that I had no idea was possible; a feeling I had only read about in magazines. My heart pounded wildly, and my body was on fire, and nothing else mattered. Not even the thought of that old "death angel" which Mama had used to keep me in check. That night ... I buried *that* death angel!

I hid my gift under my bed. I needed time. Wednesday was Mama's day off from work. I came through the door and knew immediately by that fierce look in her eyes that something was wrong, and my legs and heart froze.

Oh Lord, I thought, *I hope...*

"Georgann!" Snapped Mama, "who gave you this?" She snatched the raincoat off the bed, holding it out in front of me.

My heart began to beat rapidly. My mind became blank.

"Luke gave it to me for my birthday."

"Well you betta give it back to him and I mean soon!" She commanded, "You don't accept nothin' from 'dat boy."

"Why I gotta give it back? He gave it to me for my birthday."

"Didn't I tell you not to see 'dat boy? And you went on and disobeyed me!" said Mama. "Mama, I'm seventeen years old and you can't tell me who to like!" I knew instantly, my hormones had taken over my better sense and I had put myself on death row.

"Heifer!" yelled Mama, "Who you think you're talkin' to? I'll beat the *hell* outta you!" She grabbed me and took her house shoe off her right foot. *Mama went crazy!*

I screamed and yelled, *"Kill me! Kill me! Kill me! I don't care, 'cause you can't pick nobody for me!"*

Apparently, I had read too many of those magazines and looked at too much television, and had gotten fictional stories confused with real-life, "black folks" drama. Mama threw that shoe down and grabbed me by my dress collar. Her cafe' short order cooking, dishwashing worn hand, that had lovingly rubbed my stomach...trying to comfort my monthly complaints, now, was balled into a fist about to put some "sho nuff" *hurt* on me!

Oh Jesus! Mama really is gonna kill me!

Suddenly Mama's hands were at her side. Angry, hurt, and baffled, the emotions filled her eyes.

Breathing hard she gasped, "Gurl, I betta 'git outta this house 'fore I *kill* you!" Mama grabbed her purse and swiftly rushed out the door, slamming it behind her.

I fell across my bed and cried hysterically, when suddenly I heard familiar footsteps on that old wooden front porch. My body stiffened. I thought, *Oh no, please don't let this be Daddy!*

The door opened and there stood this six-foot four-inch tree of a man. The blood vessels in Daddy's forehead were popping out.

"Georgann!" yelled Daddy, "what's this yo' grandmama tellin' me about you sass-mouthin' her?"

"Daddy, I wasn't sassin' back to her," I replied, "I was just lettin' her know that she can't run my life anymore."

"Oooh!" he said, "I guess because you're seventeen now you think you're grown?"

"No," I replied, my eyes looked stubbornly beyond him. "I don't think I'm grown. I just think it's time for me to make my *own* decision, who I should like!"

"Girl, yo' grandmama has done everything she can for you! She has gone without things for herself in order to get them for you, and you show her disrespect like that!" Daddy's roaming voice yelled, "I ought to *whip* yo' ass myself!"

Defiantly, I looked up at him, eye to eye. "Why should you whip me? You've never done anything for me!"

Ooh Lordy! My mouth over-loaded my ass!

Suddenly, Daddy's big eyes got even bigger and red as fire. He took off his belt, and I felt the sting of it across my butt. And for a person who cried and screamed ridiculously from the least pain...I tried to be tough. I refused to give him the satisfaction of seeing me cry.

I stared him in the eyes, and with a commanding tone, I yelled, "Daddy, don't hit me anymore!"

Daddy's eyes got blood red and almost burst from their sockets. His wide nostrils were protracting outward and inward, and he was puffing like a fire-breathing dragon. He grabbed me in the collar, and jerked me about, like a sack of potatoes. My eyes saw the knuckles of his big black fist, coming to crush my face in!

Whoa! God granted me mercy.

Daddy suddenly let go of me. He looked at me in bewilderment.

"Georgann," said Daddy, "I don't know what has gotten into you, disrespectin' yo' grandmama because of some hoodlum! What is the *matter* with you!?"

Daddy shook his head from side to side and walked out of the house.

I stood there for several minutes trying to absorb all that had taken place in the last hour. I thought, *My God! I came so close to bein' knocked out by Mama, or worse, killed by Daddy!*

I knew I had committed the worst act in my life - an unpardonable sin. I had been reared from childhood never to disrespect your parents. If so, you would never have good luck, and your days on earth would be shortened. I knew my life on earth was doomed.

Mama returned home about an hour later. We didn't talk with each other. I left home and walked up to the wrong place…The Big House. One thing about my grandmama's sisters; they could pick and pluck you apart like a chicken, cut you up, roll you in batter, fry, and serve you for Sunday dinner.

As I entered through the front door, from the kitchen, I heard old "sourpuss" Aunt Clara, whose hateful ways, couldn't keep a man no longer than John's stint in the Army. She said, "Huh! 'Dat gal jus' done gon' plum *crazy* over dat ol' boy. She must be smellin' her *piss*." She continued, "I told Olivia dat *spoiled* gal was gon' make her heart ache one day. Now she sees what I meant! If I was her, I'll put dat heifer *outta* my house!" I barely could hear Aunt Cora, the secretive, eldest, and quietest sister whose tight-lipped, plain, un-expressible face always murmured under her breath. She had six grown children but wanted to give the impression they got conceived by "Immaculate Conception." Then I heard Nannie, who gets her thrills sneaking out *in the midnight hour* with *Miz Whatshername's* husband. She said, "Georgann is a good gurl. She jus' don' let dat ol' boy *touch* her, and now she don't know how to act!" I returned home, threw myself on my bed, and cried. The entire family hated me. I felt like an outcast.

Tuesday evening after choir rehearsal, Luke was there waiting. With the box in my hands, fighting back my tears, I said, "Luke, I can't accept yo' gift. Mama told me to give it back to you."

"Why?" he asked, "Why can't you accept it?"

"She won't *let* me!" I cried, "And she said that I better not see you anymore!"

"Oh! So that's the way it is, huh?"

"Yes," I replied, in hopelessness, "My entire family is mad at me. I'd rather wait until I graduate from school and I'll be on my own, then can't anyone tell me what to do and who to like."

"Okay, Georgann, if that's the way you want it."

Luke, with a dejected look, walked off with the box under his arm. A piece of my heart went with him. With tears rolling down my cheeks, I knew I would never feel for anyone else the way I felt for him.

The next morning as I was walking to school, my attention was caught by something that looked familiar. I stopped and looked over in the ditch. There was the box that Luke had given me. I stepped closer and the raincoat was there too, all ripped apart and scattered about.

"Oh no!" I cried out, "My beautiful raincoat!" With a sinking heart, I gathered up fragments of what had been my gift, held it in my hands and cried.

I thought, *How terrible! Why would Luke rip it to threads? I didn't think my returning his gift and ending our relationship had such a devastating effect upon him, to resort to this action.*

Consequently, my concentration in the classroom was absolutely zero. I could only sit and stare out into space, reflecting upon the last meeting Luke and I had. In my over-dramatic mind, I visualized the scene of him destroying my beautiful raincoat and hat.

Saturday morning, Mama and I were at the breakfast table. "Mama," I said, "I gave Luke's gift back to him and told him that I wouldn't be seeing him anymore."

With a very pleased look on her face, she said, "Well good! Georgann, you will find a *nice* boy soon and you will like him jus' as much as you thought you liked Luke."

My mind screamed. *No! No, I won't. Mama, you just don't understand how Luke makes me feel. How my spine tingles and my body seems to melt when he holds me in his arm. How my pulse races out of control just thinking about him!*

***

On Christmas Eve, around 7:30 p.m., I visited a girlfriend about three blocks away. I wasn't in any hurry, so I walked slowly back home, thinking I didn't have anything to look forward to other than cakes and pies that weren't to be touched until Christmas day. When I entered the house, Mama said, "Georgann, Luke was here."

My heart started beating rapidly. "He was?" I said, excitedly.

"Yes," she said, "and we had a heart to heart talk."

"What did he say?"

"He acknowledged to me 'dat he had been in a gang, but was no longer in one," Mama said. "He told me dat he don' changed since seein' you, and he ain't gonna misuse you 'cause he respects and cares 'bout you."

I stood there staring at Mama with my mouth hanging open. I was flabbergasted! I thought, *My Lord! I can't believe this!*

Mama said in a somewhat saddened tone, "Georgann, he had tears in his eyes. He convinced me 'dat he was sincere. So, I gave my permission for him to see you."

"Thank you, Mama."

With a stern look in her eyes she said, "Georgann, I still don't approve of dat boy, but if he's who you wanna see, then you have my permission."

Man, oh Man! Talk about excited, I was on cloud nine! What a Christmas present!

***

The weather in the months of January and February was cold and sunny. Walking to school in it wasn't as hideous as in past winters. I never liked the cold weather—but now I welcomed it. With Mama working at night and my being left alone, that was the opportune time for Luke and me to be together. I treasured those moments whenever he came calling. We would snuggle together with me sitting in his lap, all wrapped up in his arms.

Mama's bootlegging business was affording me the opportunity to seek treatments for those monthly excruciating stomach cramps, from Dr. Clark, a gynecologist. In reminiscence, my first visited was hilarious; Dr. Clark trying to examine me. Mama was allowed to come into the room along with his nurse. I lay on the examining table in the usual manner and every time he made the effort to examine me, like a scared jack-rabbit, I would jump back farther from him. This scene was repeated several times, until he finally gave up. I was not ready for *that* experience.

Dr. Clark had said to Mama, "Georgann is not going to allow me to examine her. You can be proud of the fact that she is sixteen years old and still a virgin."

Now a year later ...Suddenly that old "death angel" resurrected from the dead. I just knew that I was pregnant and that I was going to die in labor. Of course, I pictured old *sourpuss* Aunt Clara, who could be as mean as an old dried-up cow, telling Mama, "If I was you, I would put dat *heifer* outta my house!"

"Ooh Lordy!" I cried, "please don't let me be pregnant, 'cause Mama is gonna put me out!"

On Wednesday after school, without Mama's knowledge, I was sitting in Dr. Clark's office confessing my sin.

Dr. Clark raised his eyebrows, "You're what?" he asked.

"I think I'm pregnant!" I repeated, as the tears unleashed from my eyes.

"Have you let some boy *touch* you?" He asked. Those warm blue eyes that once looked at me so kindly were now staring, piercing into mine with disappointment in them.

"Yes, sir," I mumbled, with my eyes shifting to the floor.

"Let me examine you to see what is going on here," he said.

Afterwards we went back into his office. "Georgann," he said. "I'm going to give you a shot and if you don't start your period within three days, there is a possibility that you are pregnant."

The tears flooded my eyes and ran down my cheeks.

Dr. Clark's eyes narrowed, as he stared and observed me for several minutes without speaking a word.

Why is Dr. Clark angry with me? I thought. *What does it matter to him if a poor skinny colored girl thinks that she's pregnant?*

Suddenly those disappointed eyes softened and he said, "Georgann, do you want to be a *maid* for the rest of your life?"

Looking him directly in the eyes, I answered, "No, sir."

"Well, you tell that boy to keep his *'cotton pickin'* hands off you!"

Going home on the city bus, I was in a somber mood. Many thoughts ran through my mind. I thought of how disappointed Mama would be. How I was too young to be having a baby, how I would be a high-school dropout, and for some reason, it even mattered what ol' trifin' Daddy thought.

Three days later my torment ended. I was never happier in all my life! I got down on my knees, thanking and praising God! I crossed my heart and I hoped to die that *that* frightening episode ended my *sinful ways*. However, if I had signed a document on celibacy, no sooner than the ink would had dried on the paper, it would have been voided!

***

It was a rainy, muggy day that March, and I wanted to blame that for my gloomy mood. But the truth of the matter, it was Luke's departure. One day we are inseparable...couldn't get enough of each other. And the next day Luke just vanishes. He left town suddenly, without even a goodbye.Two weeks afterward, I went to the mailbox, and there was a letter from Luke. He was in California, but he would be coming back soon. That letter put the pep back in my step. We continued our long distance courtship through letters.

May 28, 1962—the big night finally arrived. I was so excited to be marching with my classmates to receive my high school diploma. It was an honor to be included in the first graduating class of Bethune Junior and Senior High School. Mama, having a relieved and happy look on her face, allowed me to go out to a nightclub with some of my classmates. I finally got a chance to step on the floor of one of the hottest night clubs named Club 51, in the rural area of Shreveport called Cooper Road.

Chapter 6
Deaf, Dumb, and Blind

If naïve could have been packaged in a box and sealed, the name of that box would have been "Maple-Georgann."

After graduation, the $50 scholarship I had received from R&E Magnetic Beauty School on Milam Street was just a down payment. In order to finance the $200 balance, I found a job with a Linen Supply Service. I felt a sense of pride, having a job and making my own income...grown, single, and committed.

It had been a month, and my routine had not changed. I worked days, attended beauty school at night, practiced with choir on Tuesday nights, and went to church on Sundays. That behavior didn't seem to settle well with Daddy. He felt that I was letting the best years of my life pass by me.

One Saturday night, as usual, Daddy was making preparations for the night out. And I, with my usual ritual, had curled up in my bed with two, thick, freshly-made tuna sandwiches, a 16-ounce RC Cola, and my two favorite magazines, *Modern Romance* and *True Story*. Anticipating a sad story with a fairy-tale ending, I had a handkerchief to wipe the tears and snot from my face. Suddenly, I noticed Daddy glancing at me, shaking his head as if he had something on his mind. He dressed and was about to make his exit. However, he approached me hesitantly and said, "Georgann, I want to talk to you."

"What is it Daddy?"

"I know you feel that I have never done anything for you," said Daddy. "And I let your grandmother make all the decisions of how she wanted to raise you. But, I have to admit, I am proud of the way you turned out. You're a good girl!"

Daddy is proud of me!

"The only thing I am disappointed in is your choice of a boyfriend. Luke is not the right boy for you. And since he's gone, you need to get out and enjoy your life. It don't make no sense for you to sit around this house like a old woman. Get out and have fun. It's gotta be in you, cause yo' mama Essie Dell wasn't slow. And you *know* I ain't slow! So, get out of the house. Find you a nice boy. There are *plenty* of them out there!"

I tried to interrupt, but Daddy's hands went up. "Hold it, let me finish," he said calmly. "I know you think that you can change Luke. But girl, I am tellin' you from experience that is not gonna happen. You haven't experienced the real world." Daddy gave me a stare, and said, "Hell, girl! Anybody saw you walkin' down the street could tell you're a chicken ripe for the pluckin'. And Lord! With that babyish soundin' voice, it's a dead give-away." Daddy continued, "Georgann, the only things you know about life are those magazines that you read. Well, life is not like those books. Those stories are just fantasies that someone made up to sell. Everybody's life doesn't have a happy ending."

"Daddy, Luke is not like you think. He's a *good* person! He's a hard worker and he treats me with so much respect. He doesn't cuss around me and don't let his friends say bad words in my presence. He won't do anything to hurt me!" I exclaimed innocently.

Daddy threw up his hands and he shook his head, "Well Georgann, yo' grandmama and I have tried to tell you about that boy. I guess you will have to find out for yo' self." Then Daddy spoke more gently and quietly, "But if he ever laid a hand on you, he will have me to answer to! Anyway, I just want to let you know that I am proud of you."

There was a moment of silence between us. Daddy suddenly looked uncomfortable. Perhaps a little guilty or regretful because he could and should have done more. I thought, *He didn't even attend my graduation nor bought me a gift. But now he is acknowledging his pride in me! Do I forgive him? Not that he is asking for forgiveness. But he did say what I had been wishing to hear from him and never heard before. He said I have made him proud. That is music to my ears.*

I embraced my daddy.

***

The month of July, 1962 was very hot. Especially for those who couldn't afford air conditioning or window fans. We would always be thankful for any little breath of air coming through our windows, but nothing could have dampened the excitement I was feeling that Friday evening as I sat on the front porch wearing Mama's loud-scented Jungle Gardenia cologne. I was trying to catch a light breeze of air, waiting and watching patiently for Luke.

The sun gradually began fading away, and the twilight of the evening set in. Suddenly, I looked up the road and knew that familiar walk. The head held high, shoulders back straight. The certain way those arms swung. I knew that walk anywhere. It had to be Luke, with a plaid shirt and blue overalls worn with his trademark of the one strap fastened over the shoulder and the other strap hanging from the back ... walking hurriedly. My pounding heart was racing with excitement! *Luke had finally come back to me!*

Luke took me by my hands as we stood staring in each others eyes, "Baby, you don't know how much I've missed you," he said smiling.

Lost in my fairy tale world, I stared dreamily into his eyes and whispered, "I missed you too."

Yet, that same year in September, the focus in Shreveport made headlines in the Shreveport Times and Journal newspapers: An ol' hometown boy, George Wendell D'Artois, who was born December 25, 1925. He grew up on a street named St. Vincent, graduated from Byrd High School in 1942, fought in World War II, honorably discharged from the Marine Corps as a Sergeant and was elected to serve as Commissioner of Public Safety.

The majority of white folks in Shreveport thought D'Artois was the best thing happened since 1793, when Eli Whitney invented the cotton gin. The colored folks felt that D'Artois wanted to be like a slave master; cracking whip and corralling Black people into being quiet as "rats pissin' on cotton!"

***

It was January of 1963. Luke now worked with a construction company. He bought a beautiful 1955 Chevrolet car, with the gear shift in the floor. Everything was going smoothly. I definitely knew that Luke was the only man for me, and that we would get married one day. But I also knew something else; Luke liked to gamble.

Country Shack, it was called. The most notorious of all the little hole-in-the-wall juke joints in the

Mooretown section of the city. On the residential street called Carl Terrace, a block up from where another of Mama's sisters, Aunt Ida Mae Hunter and her family lived. Practically every weekend there would be some type of incident - fighting, shooting, or stabbing. You could hear the gun shots from miles away, and that honky tonk music was always blaring loud and clear. It was always crowded. And, of course, it wouldn't be a shack if it didn't have a crap-shooting room in the back for illegal gambling. Customers from all sections of our city patronized it. It was said that if you wanted to have a "funky good time", Country Shack was the place.

Throughout my eighteen years, I had always heard about Country Shack, but I had never ventured toward it. Not even those Friday and Saturday nights when I would go searching for Daddy. As desperately as I wanted to find him, I dared not go to Country Shack!

Now, on this particular Saturday morning, Daddy, Mama and I were sitting at the table eating breakfast. Daddy, with a smug look on his face, said arrogantly, "Oh, by the way Georgann, *that* boyfriend of yours was at Country Shack last night and got put in jail."

"What did he do?" I asked.

"For gambling," Daddy's eyes bucked. "I told you that hoodlum boy ain't no good, but you won't listen!" He added, "I be around him and his friends a lot of times without him realizing I'm there, and I know how he be actin'!"

I sat there, getting more disheartened with his accusations of Luke, when soft-hearted Mama interjected, "Leave the gurl alone, George. Caint you see she's upset?"

Daddy said, "Somebody needs to open up her eyes about *that* boy!"

Luke and I dated about two years. During those years Luke was frequently arrested for either gambling or getting traffic violations and not paying them. I had glaring warning signs, but I refused to recognize them, because I was going to change Luke's behavior. I had proof it could be done, from reading all those love stories in the magazines. The "good girls" always changed the boys from those bad habits.

Mama was like a prosecuting attorney, arguing her case. She warned, "Georgann, I know what you think you're gonna do, and 'dat is *change Luke*. But 'dat ain't gon' happen! You've always had yo' way, and 'dat's partly my fault. But chile, I'm tellin' you, you is bitin' off mo' than you can chew!"

"But Mama", I whined, "I *can* help Luke to change!"

Mama's eyes stretched, and she said, "If his *own* Mama couldn' do nothin' wit' him, what makes you think you can!?" Mama continued, "Gurl, you caint git blood outta a turnip! It just ain't in him. Luke is gonna *sour* on yo' stomach!"

Even Mrs. Minnie, Luke's mother, with her eyes squinted, pointed her finger at me. "Gurl!" she said, "I hope you know what you're doing!"

Nonetheless, on December 19, 1964, fourteen days after my twentieth birthday, I carried on the family tradition of having my wedding at the Big House. The family, in spite of their disapproval, contributed to the festivities, even Aunt Clara.

Daddy reluctantly gave me away.

My grandmama gave me the "Good Book."

"Here Chile," she said, "you gonna be needin' this!"

I was surprisingly calm, standing beside Luke in my white suit, holding my new bible in my hands, looking all prim, proper, and sanctimonious. I was ready to conquer the unimaginable, not realizing that I was ill prepared and unequipped for the world that I was about to enter.

Chapter 7
What's in you, gonna come out

Our little duplex apartment in Mooretown on a street called Lucille couldn't have been more perfect. Those freshly painted walls, the new linoleum covering on the floors, and brand new furniture for every room, were simply beautiful. Even the location was convenient, about a block up from my church which was on the corner of Hollywood and Lucille Street. As that saying goes, "A family that prays together, stays together." I had formed the image of Luke and me walking those few steps to church on Sunday mornings.

Luke was now working for a trucking company with good pay. I quit my job with the Linen service and put Beauty School on hold to become a full-time housewife. It took no extraordinary effort for me to rise out of bed on those early mornings to prepare Luke's breakfast and lunch. That same effort was given later in the evenings. I listened for Luke's car, with that loud muffler. The instant I heard it, the water for his bath was run. And Friday's were special... payday. Luke and I had a routine; together we went to the bank to cash his check, paid our bills, and off to the supermarket.

I didn't object when Luke went out on weekends. There were times I helped him dress; had his clothes laid on the bed for him; shined his shoes. I saw no problem with a man having worked hard all week, going out and unwinding with the guys on Friday and Saturday nights, as long as Luke had taken care of his financial responsibilities. In hindsight, I guess one could say I was like the characters in that movie called, "The Stepford Wives", only I required the husband to bring his money home to me and I would manage it. I had worked out a durable regimen and all Luke had to do was follow the plan. I had thought Luke was in compliance with that arrangement, until one day Mama cautioned.

"Georgann," said Mama, "Luke says you take's all his money and jus' give him a nuff money to put gas in his car, and a few dollars extra."

Surprisingly I answered, "But Mama, that's all Luke needs," I replied. "Because I make sure all the bills are paid, and I buy his cigarettes when we go to the market. What more could he ask for?"

Mama shook her head and warned, "Georgann, you shouldn't take all the man's money."

I brushed it off, "Aah Mama." I said, "Luke doesn't need any more money."

But I did.

In March of 1965, I returned to beauty school to complete my course. Only forty hours were needed for the Testing Board, and a payment balance of fifty dollars on my tuition. The Board was meeting within two months. With careful budgeting, I could save the fifty dollars.

Luke and I were a team. I made the rules and he was following them. And so far, everything was going smoothly. But somewhere within that third month things changed; I became pregnant and Luke gradually started breaking the rules. Instead of Luke coming directly home to get me, he went to the bank alone, cashed his check and brought me the money and the check stub. I thought, *Okay, I could live with this.* However, several weeks later, the check stub didn't balance out with the money.

"Luke," I questioned. "What happened to the rest of the money?"

"Georgann, I got a speedin' ticket," said Luke. "And I had to pay it."

Luke's 1955 Chevy hot-rod was built for drag racing.But instead of racing it at the Drag Strip on weekends, Luke drag raced on the public streets, getting speeding tickets frequently. I was still doing my "Stepford Wife" routine, making it as comfortable and convenient for Luke as possible.

Luke also had the conveniences of what I soon discovered was not a recreational gambling habit; Country Shack was a street over...and Lord have mercy! My carefully planned budget became non-existent, and the bills began to mount. I completed the hours necessary to get my Beautician's License. But I could save no money. We got a loan for $150. That Friday evening when we arrived home with the money, Luke, calling me by the pet name he had given me, said, "Ann, let me keep the money 'til Monday, you don't need it until then."

Suspiciously, I asked, "Why do you want to keep it?"

"I just want to keep it." He said, "Don't you trust me?"

I looked into his eyes and felt guilty as I said within myself, "No, I don't."

I hesitated, but then said, "Alright, you can keep it. But please don't gamble this money away!"

"Ann, do you think I'm *crazy*?" He said. "I know what we gotta do with this money, and I ain't gonna mess it up!"

Reluctantly, I gave Luke the $150.

Three hours passed. I sat at the window watching for Luke like a hawk. One o'clock Saturday morning Luke came home.

"Georgann, I'm so sorry!" said a teary-eyed Luke. "Please forgive me!"

"Luke! What happened? You didn't lose the money?"

Luke shook his head, saying, "I lost all the money!"

My opened mouth froze.

However, love is supposed to conquer all. I gathered Luke in my arms. "Don't cry...it's gonna be alright."

"But Ann," he said sorrowfully. "Monday you s'posed to pay the money, and I done lost it!"

"I can take the test next year." While trying to console Luke and thinking, *Lord, don't let this one incident cause me to give up on him. Help me to have love, patience, and understanding.*

Meanwhile, putting that one gambling incident behind us, I was a contented pregnant wife, and everything seemed to be going great.

However, the real Luke could only play that part for so long. Luke's coming home from work on Friday's got later and later, and the money was coming up shorter and shorter. It was gradually developing into a pattern, until the dreadful inevitable...he didn't come home. That's when the "shit hit the fan," and I went ballistic.

It was a Friday evening. I was in my sixth month of pregnancy and I had looked forward to showing off my prettiest maternity dress for Luke, but he didn't show up.

I got undressed, went to bed, and cried myself to sleep. Saturday morning, Luke still had not come home. I began making telephone calls. No one had seen him. Finally, about one o'clock in the afternoon, Luke came home.

"Luke, where have you been?" I asked.

"I was just 'round to Country Shack."

"Country Shack," I repeated, "all night?!"

"Yeah, I got into a little gamblin' game," he explained. "I got another speedin' ticket and I wanted to win the money back that I had used to pay the ticket wit."

"Did you win it back?"

Luke hesitated then said, "Naw, I lost it all!"

I stared at him with utter disbelief. Suddenly, a pregnancy tantrum emerged and that dark side of me exposed itself. Those main ingredients that I prayed for-love, patience, and understanding- momentarily escaped my memory. I made teeth-prints in Luke's chest! I bit him...I hit him...and I tried to kick him!

Luke overpowered me and finally got me calmed down.

The thought of being homeless, or having to eat pinto beans and biscuits everyday, didn't set too well.

Sobbing, I asked, "What are we gonna do about our rent and food?"

"Don't worry about it. I will get the money to buy food." Luke said, with confidence. "We'll just have to pay the rent next week. Let me handle it."

Luke left home and returned hours later with a wad of one-dollar bills. The appearance of that money was wrinkled and had the odor of cigarette smoke on it. It was obviously gambling money. I became very familiar with that offensive odor on those dollar bills and in his clothing, not fully realizing it came with the territory.

I felt that I was slowly being thrust into an unfamiliar life ... a whole new environment. I realized I had to grow up and be very responsible if we were to have a good marriage. Because of his squandering ways it was going to be left totally on my shoulders to make it work, until the glorious day when Luke would magically change.

The J. C. Penney's lay-a-way paper showed a balance of $10. That cold, November Thursday afternoon, I was at the Big House showing Mama the slip of paper that named all the items I had on layaway. Mama gasped, "Georgann! 'dat baby ain't gon' need all this stuff to start out wit'!"

"But Mama", I said, "I want to have everything that's going to be needed now, so that I won't have to worry about it later. Besides, we can afford it, 'cause Luke got a good payin' job wit' that trucking company." I boasted, "He makes $70 a week."

Mama's eyes widened, "$70 a week!" Mama repeated. "Chile, dat's some *good* money. Now don't spend every penny. You need to save some for a rainy day."

I thought to myself, *Mama don't realize that every week can become a rainy day with Luke!*

Two weeks later, on that Friday evening, our little apartment was sparkling clean, as I awaited Luke's arrival from work. Seven o'clock I was still waiting for Luke. Eight o'clock...I was still waiting for Luke. By 9 p.m., every car with a loud muffler coming down Lucille Street, I tried to *will* those cars to be Luke's car. Around 10 p.m., seven months pregnant and waddling like a duck on that chilly Friday night, I stood at the door on the outside of Country Shack. I was embarrassed, on the verge of tears, and asking anybody and everybody to summon my husband. I considered myself a nice respectable Christian, and going into a place of that sort was beneath me. But it was more befitting to stand on the outside and act liked the beggar! Finally, some good "Samaritan" made contact.

"Georgann, what you doin' here?" asked Luke.

"I'm here because you didn't come home. And I hope you haven't messed up the money!"

Luke was hyped. His eyes were dancing around in his head, and he was talking fast. "Naw Ann, I ain't lost the money. I'm on a winnin' streak!"

"Luke," I begged. "Please don't lose the money, 'cause you promised that we would get the baby's things out of lay-a-way, tomorrow!"

"Ann, we've got plenty of time before the lay-a-way hafta be out." Then Luke, in his cunning ways grabbed my arms, kissed my cheek for reassurance and said, "Now, you go on back home and I'll be on as soon as I hit this big win!" Luke came home about five o'clock Saturday morning, with barely enough money for groceries.

It became apparent that Luke's word meant diddly-squat! I was getting a rude awakening. My fantasy of the "hard working man" who takes care of his family didn't quite represent Luke. Work presented no problem for Luke, but he had problems being responsible with money! Not only that, I got another eye opener...Luke's ability to read was very limited. But that was not going to be an obstacle to my plan. Mama's wedding gift...she had said I was going to need it. She didn't lie! ... Luke and I had Bible Study.

On January 25, 1966, Jeff was born. Three months later, Mama babysat Jeff, while I returned to Beauty School. Six weeks later, I finally got my license and started working at a beauty parlor within walking distance from the house.

For several months, it seemed that things were going well. Luke was home on weekends more and did well with his financial obligations. I saw a glimmer of hope!

But soon, Luke made me realize that I had had no business trying to impersonate the "potter," because he certainly wasn't going to continue imitating the "clay." One Friday Luke went to work and didn't return. I had had enough of Luke! Six o'clock on Saturday evening, Daddy helped me load Jeff's baby bed with all our belongings. Before the crack of dawn Sunday morning, a longing and tugging at my heart for Luke and our little three-room apartment found me tiptoeing to the telephone.

"Hello." Luke answered in a drowsy voice.

"Luke," I whispered into the telephone. "I wanna come home!"

"OK Ann. Gimme time to get my clothes on and I'll be there."

Shamed-faced, I couldn't look Mama in her eyes. "Mama," I said, "Luke is comin' to get me."

"What?" Mama yelled. "Chile, giv'da boy a nuff time to *miss* you!" she continued, "He jus' might *straighten up and fly right*!"

Looking down, I said, "I wanna go back home to Luke."

Mama shrugged her shoulders, shook her head and said, "Georgann, it ain't no sense in you bein' *dat* bigga fool!"

"Girl!" said Daddy. "You had me borrow a car, take that baby's crib apart, load all that stuff, and now you talkin' about going *back*," said an angry Daddy. "Well, don't expect me to help you anymore!"

Nannie puffed on her cigarette and strangled. Her eyes stretched the size of two fifty-cent coins as they rolled to the ceiling. "Gurl!" she gasped. "You love dat boy's *dirty* drawers!"

After all was said, it didn't have any measure over my love. Luke came and got Jeff and me. We were back in our castle!

Chapter 8
Daddy was Warned

Miz Luvenia, who lived in a white house on the corner of Jewella and Faye Street probably wasn't known throughout the Shreveport area. But she was well known in the little community of Stills Quarters. She was the self-proclaimed coroner for the community.

It was smothering hot that June of 1968. The doctor had made a house call early Thursday morning to the Big House. Shaking his head and saying, "There isn't anything I can do for her. It's just a matter of time." Two years before, Aunt Clara, with a frown on her face, had gone to meet her Maker. Now, Nannie's sickness had finally taken its toll. Late that evening, family and friends gathered at the Big House. We crowded around Nannie's bed in silence. Around seven o'clock, the mirror was covered as Nannie's eyes took on a faded look. I softly kissed Nannie's forehead and held her hand as she peacefully took her last deep breath.

Teary-eyed, Mama quietly spoke, "Georgann, go 'git Luvenia."

Those bow legs of Miz Luvenia's moved quickly as we made those few steps out of her back door into the back door of the Big House. Miz Luvenia was all business when she felt Nannie's pulse, put her ears to Nannie's chest, and raised Nannie's eyelids.

Nannie gave no response.

Miz Luvenia nodded her head, indicating life on this side had ended for Nannie. She closed Nannie's opened eyes, and placed a nickel over each eye.

Everybody was grieved.

J.S. Williams' hearse came and carried Nannie's body away.

Time moves on and changes come. Within that same year of 68, the "Godfather of Soul", James Brown, wrote and recorded the song *Say It Loud, I'm Black & I'm Proud*. I don't know whether James Brown's record lit a *fire* under Daddy's *ass* or what got into Daddy because he went *looney tooney*!

In August, our church membership had outgrown its building and needed a larger place to worship. The once white congregational building, Emmanuel Baptist Church, on the corner of a street named Tate and Jewella Avenue, became Morning Star Baptist Church. Several months later, our beloved pastor, Reverend Woodson, passed away. Our old church building on Hollywood Avenue had been sold to a white man named Stanley Lewis, owner of Stan's Record Shop on downtown Texas Street. Mister Stanley Lewis did the unthinkable.

Mama's eyes bucked with fear and she pitched a fit. "George!" she gasped, "you must be don' gon' *stone* crazy!"

"Olivia, I'm just gonna be the manager. It not gonna be like a juke joint where liquor is sold," said Daddy.

"But George," cried Mama, *"It's terrible, jus' terrible!!* You don't turn a church buildin' dats been dedicated to God into a pool hall," said Mama. "Dat's sacrilegious!"

"Aw, Olivia," said Daddy. "You worry too much!"

Mama shook her finger in Daddy's face and said, "George, mark my words, God is gonna *git* you!"

Influential ministers warned Daddy that his actions were dangerous and that God was not pleased by them. *Daddy didn't give a shit!* Daddy felt by being a manager, for the first time in his life, he wouldn't have the *white man* breathing down his neck, giving him orders, as was in the Navy; "boy do this, boy do that." Now he would be The Man! But Mama said her son had lost sight of *who sits high and looks low!* ... And you don't disrespect HIS house!

Even I was scared for Daddy. Upon impulse, I stepped into my old church building and what was once the place where a pulpit and pews were, there were now, pool tables. Instead of a piano and choir singing praises to God, there was a juke box. I found it very uncomfortable. I only visited twice. That last visit, I found my daddy and a stranger sitting at a table gambling.

The stranger threw the cards down hard to the table.

Daddy's eyes bucked, and he used a word that I had never before heard him use, "Well I'll be a motherfucka!" he said.

I was shocked and gasped, "Daddy!"

Daddy, who didn't realize my presence, had a sheepish look on his face, and apologized. "I'm sorry Georgann."

"George, yo' daughter must don't know you very well," said the snickering stranger.

I was horrified!

I said in a whisper, "Oh my God! Daddy is desecrating the Lord's house!" Thinking the ceiling was going to crash down on our heads, I grabbed Jeff and my feet couldn't carry me out of there fast enough! I thought, *not only do I pray for Luke, but I need to pray for Daddy too!*

My spontaneous one night separation from Luke did not produce lasting changes in his actions. Luke returned to his old irresponsible behavior. Bill collectors were calling on Monday because Luke didn't pay the bills that past Friday. His inconsistency was causing chaos, and my beauty business wasn't thriving as anticipated. I needed a steady income.

In April of 1969, I landed a job with Western Electric, a manufacturing company. Two months later Luke's company transferred to Dallas, Texas. But Luke immediately found a job with a construction company, building homes. We moved out of the duplex and rented a house.

***

August 18, 1969: It was a sunny and beautiful day that afternoon at work. I couldn't imagine why I was being summoned by the security officer to come to the guard gate. Luke was waiting there with a gloomy expression on his face. He took me by my arm. "Let's get in the car."

"What's the matter?" I questioned.

"Just get in the car."

I got into the car with a sinking feeling in my stomach, and my heart seemed like it was put on hold.

Luke took a deep breath, and said, "Yo' Daddy got shot."

"Shot!" I yelled, as the most devastating feeling I had ever experienced in my entire life came over me.

Suddenly, it dawned on me; he didn't say dead. Hope sprung up. "Well, he is going to be all right, isn't he?"

"No Ann," he said with reluctance, "He's dead!"

My heart sank.

"Oh no!" I screamed repeatedly. *"My daddy couldn't be dead... Not my Daddy!"*

Luke grabbed me and held me tightly, trying to comfort me. I sat in silence hoping that this was all a nightmare and I would awaken. At the Big House, family members were seated on the lawn, grieving. I walked over to Mama, who wasn't showing any emotions, yet had the most strange and painful look on her face. I touched her and it went unnoticed, as if I were not present. She was in shock.

Daddy must have been on a collision course with death. In the midst of my grief, I couldn't help but reflect on a month earlier when Mama had made that long walk from the Big House to visit me unexpectedly. She was blazing hot as she entered the front door.

"Mama! What's the matter?" I asked.

"Georgann, 'dat Daddy of yo's like to made me kill'im!" she said.

"What did he do?"

"I was tellin' him about helpin' wit' payin' some of the bills, and we got into a argument. And he had the *audacity* to ball his fist and draw it back at me!"

"I gasped out, "Oh no, Mama!"

"Yes!" Mama said, as her balled-fist went up in the air, she continued, "And I pick up 'dat big heavy ashtray on the chifforobe and I said, "Come on! And I'll *free* you from yo' sins!"

"Oh Mama!" I cried, "What's gettin' wrong wit' Daddy?"

Mama's eyes stretched big, and behind that angry look I saw hurt and disbelief.

"I don't know chile," said Mama. "But I looked him dead in the eye and pointed my finger at him, and I warned him, "George, mark my words ... You will not live out the rest of yo' days, 'cause of yo' *disrespectful ways!*"

So be it. At the age of forty-four, Daddy was shot dead on the sidewalk of Hollywood Avenue by the snickering stranger with whom he had gambled with.

Daddy's funeral took place at Morning Star Church with its new pastor, Reverend C. L. Townsel, officiating. Daddy was put away nicely. Mama had made sure of that. As funerals would be, many words of expressions were spoken about Daddy's likeable and charming personality.

In between my emotional outbursts as I sat in front of my daddy's casket, I could only reflect on his positive effects in my life. I remembered when I was about nine years old. One Saturday, Daddy went shopping and returned home, and had bought me a brand new outfit; a pair of blue jeans, a red sweater, and a pair of shoes. I could barely keep still from excitement as Mama combed my hair and put red and blue ribbons on each plait. Daddy was taking me to see my first John Wayne movie. I felt proud as he took my little hand in his, guiding me up the balcony for "coloreds only" at the Strand Theatre. I carried my bag of popcorn while he carried our Cokes. I felt at that moment, I was Daddy's little girl! As a result of that special occasion, I was a John Wayne fan forever.

After Daddy's death, Mama was never the same. I guess nothing could ease the pain of losing her child. Even if perhaps their relationship at times had been rocky and she had predicted his death. The pain would be forever there. As for me, I never realized just how much I really loved my ol' *trifin'* Daddy and as time went by I missed him so much.

Chapter 9
Was it Miz Kizzy or My Faith?

Several months passed and I was gradually getting adjusted to Daddy's death, when Luke came home one Friday with a horse... and no money! Luke had stopped drag racing. Now he wanted to horse race! I threw both hands in the air, saying "Lord, what's next?" That question didn't go unanswered for long.

Luke started having late night visitors...two suspicious looking characters. Luke would leave with them and be away for hours. I was inquisitive. Luke assured me that there wasn't anything "shady" going on, but even an ol' "dumb-dumb" like me could tell something wasn't on the up and up.

In that year of 1970, one morning, around 2 a.m., Luke left with his "partners in crime", and they were caught stealing money orders from a local store and cashing them over in Texas. Of course, Luke denied having taken the money orders. He had only provided the transportation. However, the F.B.I. had a money order with his name written on it. He and the two guys were charged with a federal offense. His bond was $2,500, which meant $250 cash to get him out on bail. Luke had been incarcerated about a month. The situation looked bleak.

That Saturday afternoon, I could tell by those stolen glances from Mama that she had something on her mind. Finally, she quietly spoke, "Georgann," said Mama. "I know a lady who could 'git Luke outta jail."

I thought, *Oh Lord! Here comes Mama with this hoodoo mess!*

"Mama, what woman you know can help get Luke out of jail?" I asked, unbelievingly.

"Well, there is this lady over in Texas who can help you," she said with assurance.

"What is she, some voodoo woman?" I responded arrogantly.

Mama said patiently, "No Georgann, she's a strong Christian lady, who believes in prayer and faith. She is a Pentecostal minister 'dat God gave a special gift to."

My ears jumped in alert: "strong Christian lady, God gave a special gift!" That aroused my interest.

"Mama," I said quickly, "What can she do and how much is it going to cost?"

"She usually charges $100."

My eyes bucked and I yelled, "*One hundred dollars!*"

"Yes, Georgann," said Mama. "But her work is guaranteed. As long as you do exactly what she tells you to do."

"But, if she's such a Christian lady that believes in helpin' people, why does she charge people?"

"Chile," said Mama. *"Dat woman gotta make a livin'!"*

After penny pinching, skimping on groceries, and doing whatever it took, four weeks later, I had saved the $100. Early that Saturday morning, with trembling knees and sweaty palms, I drove down the highway to Marshall, Texas, along with Mama and her sister.

Scared and nervous, my heart pounded loud and fast. I thought, *Oh Lord! What is that woman going to tell me to do? Is she gonna have a rabbit foot for me to put in Luke's sock and have me bury it under my steps? Some old hoodoo mess! Well, whatever she tells me, I guess I'll be willin' to try if it means gettin' Luke's freedom.*

Approximately forty minutes later, we arrived and were greeted by the lady's son. As I glanced around the living room, immediately I was drawn to objects I felt had some significant spiritual connotations; the display of Jesus, the Bible, and other objects that represented Christianity.

Finally, the lady entered the room. She looked to be in her fifties, tall and stout, and brown complexioned with a beautiful smile. But something seemed to be wrong with her right eye. I didn't want to be caught staring, but I thought, *If she can perform miracles, why can't she fix her eye?*

She greeted Mama and her sister with a hug, saying how good it was to see them...again.

Mama said, "Miz Kizzy, this is my granddaughter, Georgann."

She took my trembling hands in hers, holding them gently. "Chile don't be afraid, I'm not going to hurt you. I'm here to help you." Her eyes pierced mine, as if she could see right into my heart, through my eyes. She asked, "Are you a Christian?"

"Yes ma'am."

"Do you believe that God can perform miracles?"

"Yes ma'am."

"Well, come on back to this room, and we shall get down to business."

She led me to her special sacred room. We sat down at a small table with a Bible on it that was placed in the middle of the room.

She asked, "Georgann, do you have faith in God?"

Without any hesitancy, I answered, "Yes ma'am."

Miz Kizzy prayed. Afterward, she opened the Bible to 1 Corinthians chapter 12. "Chile," she said, "read verses 8-10 aloud."

I acted in obedience.

Miz Kizzy's hands felt warm and secure as they enfolded my hands. "Chile, do you believe what you read?" she asked.

"Yes ma'am. I believe it."

Miz Kizzy then gave me seven small sheets of onion skin paper. "Now Chile, you write down on this paper what you want God to do for you. And that is to get your husband free. Now be sure to write it down seven times on each sheet of paper for seven nights, right before you pray and get into bed. Be sure to keep the papers in your Bible." She commanded. "Now I got somethin' else to give to you."

Miz Kizzy went over to her cabinet and in her hand was a tiny bottle. "Here Chile, take this bottle of oil. Anoint a symbol of the cross on your husband's undershirt when he goes to court. Make sure he wears that anointed undershirt when he stands before the judge." She instructed.

I didn't have the nerves to ask. But I wondered, *is this hoodoo oil?*

That night, I started doing as Miz Kizzy had instructed me. After Luke had been in jail for three months, I received my vacation pay and paid his bond. He was freed on bond and his trial never came up. The other two men that were with him received sentences of two years.

Luke was very fortunate he got his job back. After having been in confinement, I just knew that situation would bring about a change in Luke. I convinced myself that he would stop his old street habits and finally be the husband I felt he could be...the kind I wanted. I thought if God could prevent Luke from going to jail, I just knew He could change Luke! It never dawned on me, to use that same method which was used to get Luke's freedom, to get him to change. Perhaps...who knows?

***

January of 1971: Jeff was now a thriving five-year-old, who was the spitting image of Luke, and I was expecting our second child. In July of that same year, we purchased our first home on a street called Cleveland. It was a neat, medium-sized house with two bedrooms, one bath, a living room, kitchen, and a big utility room. I was very excited about having our own home. Luke was especially excited with that little storage house in the back yard.

Our first weekend in our home, Luke got up early that Saturday morning and cleaned out the storage house. He swept, mopped the floor, boarded-up the two windows with plywood, and ran an outside electric extension cord from the house into the storage house.

"Luke," I asked. "Why are you cleanin' out this old storage house?"

"My friends are comin' over tonight," he answered. "And we are gonna have our rodeo club meetin'."

I thought, *Humm...that would be nice.*

That night at 7 o'clock, the meeting began. After about two hours, some of the men left and some stayed. Around 12 o'clock, I got suspicious. Standing on the outside of that little storage house, what I heard made my blood boil. I said in a whisper, "oh, hell no!"

I rushed back into the house, and I threw a "monkey wrench" in his game!

Within seconds, Luke burst through the back door, eyes bucking and looking crazy. "What happened to the light?" Luke yelled.

"You're not bringing gamblin' here, and you can tell yo' buddies I said so!" I spoke firmly. "I can't stop what you do out in those streets, but I can stop you from bringin' it into our home!"

Luke grabbed the cord from my hand and plugged it back into the socket. "Ain't no gamblin' going on out there. We're just talking," said Luke. "Now, don't you touch this plug." He went out the door, back to his gambling buddies.

I snatched the plug out of the socket, again.

Luke was furious. "Didn't I tell you to leave that plug alone!" he yelled.

"I'm not leavin' it alone!" I yelled, "Because, you are not bringing gamblin' here, and I meant that!"

Luke tried to grab the cord out of my hand. But I was determined to stand my ground, even at the risk of going into labor. Luke finally overpowered me, looked me fiercely into my eyes and said, "I'm leavin' here. If I can't have no say-so in my *own* house, then I don't need to be here!" Luke left and returned the next day.

***

On the 20th day of September 1971, I delivered a beautiful, healthy boy, named Carl.

Six weeks later, I returned to work, leaving Carl with a babysitter.

In the meantime, Luke's horse came to a fatal accident by a car. That was the end of his rodeo days. He took on another interest.

Chapter 10
The Street Hustler

It was 1972, and the movie, "Super Fly" came out. The main character, Priest, was a street hustling pimp who dealt cocaine. Priest was flamboyant; the flashy wardrobe, the stack-heeled shoes, and the Cadillac car with the gangster white-wall tires. For some, life-imitating art had become trendy.

It seemed to have gotten started in Dallas, Texas. Luke had two brothers who lived there. They made frequent trips back and forth to Shreveport in their big, fancy cars with flashy women, and would have large sums of money. To my surprise, Luke bought another car. A nice sharp used Lincoln Continental, with big gangster white-wall tires like his brothers.

Through the years, I had gotten accustomed to Luke staying out on Friday nights and coming home early Saturday mornings. I was still trying to maintain my "Stepford Wife" routine. When Luke came in, I prepared him a big breakfast of homemade biscuits, grits and bacon... like he was "the king." But gradually, Luke's Saturday mornings became evenings, and evenings became night, until it was the entire weekend.

That Sunday morning around 5:00 a.m., leaving Jeff and Carl asleep, I combed the streets of Mooretown, trying to spot Luke's car. No luck. Having used all my resources, thinking the worst, I called the Police Station. He wasn't there. Suddenly Dallas, Texas, popped up in my head. I called his brother's place and there was Luke. I was hurt and outraged.

About midnight, Luke rushed through the door. "Ann," said Luke. "I'm so sorry. Please forgive me!"

"Luke!" I snapped, and I asked the most absurd question, "How can you go off to Dallas an entire weekend without tellin' me?"

"Aw, Ann, I was just over there wit my brothers. They gonna buy me a dump truck so that I can start my own dirt hauling business." Luke continued, "I know that I was wrong for not tellin' you. And I promise to never again go to Dallas and not tell you."

I knew how Luke kept promises, but after nine years of marriage, Luke could still "rock my world!" He took me in his arms and my feelings of anger and hurt diminished.

***

It was July 1974. Mama was never the same agile person after Daddy's death. On that Saturday morning, the thirteenth, Mama became very ill, and was hospitalized for testing. I left her there, feeling sure that everything would be all right.

Sunday morning, I was summoned to the hospital. Mama was in the Intensive Care Unit and was hooked up to a heart machine. I hurried to her bedside.

The doctor said, "I'm sorry, but we've done all we can for your grandmother, her heart is just too weak."

I looked at her lying there, dying before my eyes. *I just brought her here yesterday, and today she is dying?*

I took Mama's cold hand in mine as the tears fell from my eyes. I looked at the flat line that immediately formed on the electrocardiogram machine and got the emptiest feeling that one could imagine. I remembered as a small child, Mama would leave me with one of her sisters, I would always be afraid that she would not return, leaving me abandoned. Now at the age of sixty-seven, Mama was really gone. I was devastated.

I drove home in a daze, trying to grasp and cope with Mama's death. It was so sudden. A knot formed in my throat as I tried, unsuccessfully, to hold back the tears. My Grandmama, my mama, my anchor!

Sitting quietly in my bedroom, I thought about those midnights when Mama came home from work, clothes smelling of hamburgers and fries, and hands that had the scent of dishwashing disinfectant. She wearily stayed up long hours, rubbing my stomach...nursing my complaints.

My grandmother's life had been full of disappointment, more than I could imagine. But the one thing that made her most proud was at my graduation night. She couldn't stop smiling!

I thought about all the sacrifices Mama had made in order for me to have a better life than herself. Did I ever thank her? Did I ever tell her I loved her? Guilt consumed me, like a rushing tidal wave.

Crying and sobbing, the tears spilled from my eyes. *Oh Mama, If I could just see the joy in your eyes again! Oh Mama, to touch your face and say, "I love you Mama." What a joy that would be!*

But Mama, I can't remember saying those words...I didn't say those words.

Oh Mama, dear Mama. Please hear me, "I love you Mama! I love you!"

I missed my grandmama. Her death left an empty spot in my heart that could not be filled.

***

That same year of 74, D'Artois made headlines again, third term re-elected Public Safety Commissioner. He had to "up the anti"; control those dope-pushers! And unbeknownst to me, he had a particular one on the list:

Luke's promises meant nothing. On weekends, Luke burned up those rubber tires, driving to Dallas, Texas. It was a rarity for him to be in town, with the exception of that Friday night, a night that "Dummie" could have been stamped on my forehead, and it wouldn't have been a lie!

As always, after putting in a full week at Western Electric, I saved my house cleaning for Friday nights. I was in the midst of my chores, when I heard those loud knocks at the front door. Bang! Bang! Bang!

"Who is it?" I yelled out.

"It's the Police!" he answered. "Open the door!"

There at my door were two plain clothes and a uniformed officer, staring me in my face.

The one that identified himself as a lieutenant said, "Does Luke Dunbar live here?"

Yes," I answered. "But he's not here!"

"Are you his wife?"

"Yes!"

"Well, we have a search warrant for this house."

"Search Warrant!" I repeated, "For what?"

He didn't answer, but commanded me to sit down in the living room, while they ransacked my home; looked in my closets, under mattresses, searched my medicine cabinet and kitchen cabinets.

The lieutenant confronted me, "Mrs. Dunbar, we would like to look in your purse."

The uniformed officer emptied the contents of my purse on my dining table, and confiscated a prescribed bottle of muscle relaxers. Then slowly it dawned on me, *Drugs! They are looking for drugs!*

The polite Lieutenant asked, "Mrs. Dunbar, are there any balloons in the house?"

"No." I answered, while thinking, *what balloons have to do with this?*

Suddenly, eight-year-old Jeff burst out innocently, "Yes, sir."

The lieutenant said, "Show me son."

Jeff led the way into our bedroom. He pulled out Luke's drawer from the dresser, and to my surprise, there were balloons. I was dumbfounded.

They gathered the balloons and the lieutenant suddenly apologized. "Mrs. Dunbar, we are sorry to have disrupted your house and disturbed you." He paused, then said "You keep a clean house Mrs. Dunbar." They left.

I dropped in the chair, stunned.

The time on the clock wasn't moving fast enough. I couldn't wait to confront Luke. Hours later, I said calmly, "Luke, the police have been here."

Luke's eyes rolled around. "What did they want?"

"They had a search warrant and evidently were searching for drugs. Why would they want to search our house?"

"Because of my brothers in Dallas", said Luke. "They just want to harass me!"

My hands went to my hips and my head stuck out. "Luke, I am not gonna tolerate drugs in *this* house! *Me* and *my children* will not be exposed to that type of lifestyle!"

Luke, who knew how to pull my chain and stroke my ego, said, "Do you think I'm crazy? I know you ain't the kind of woman that'd put up wit that." He continued, "My brothers even said the reason they won't allow me to get involved in their business is because of you. They said if they had a wife like you, they wouldn't be into drugs."

Luke's slick-talking and convincing ways were like throwing feed to a hungry chicken that could easily be plucked, and figuratively, I was covered with chicken feathers. However, that following month, my body literally felt covered.

It was a weird feeling. It felt to be crawling all over my body. Yet, it seemed to be in one particular area. I submerged it in the hottest temperature of water that I could bear. I washed it. I scrubbed it. I scratched it. But nothing could stop the itch. I thought, *what the hell is this?* I looked. It couldn't be seen with the naked eye. I grabbed my small hand mirror. I saw them... crawling...I screamed to the top of my lungs..."LUKE!"

Luke ran into the bathroom. "Ann, what's wrong?"

"Somethin' is on me!"

"Well, what is it?"

"I don't know." I said. "You look and see!"

Luke made his inspection, raised an eyebrow, and spoke calmly. "Oh, them just crabs. It's nothin' to hurt you."

"How in the world did I get this?" I yelled. "I couldn't have gotten it from anyone but you! And how did you get it?"

Luke stuttered, "Ah, ah...the job I'm doin' makes me sweat so much and the dirt mixed wit that sweat cause crabs to come on me," said Luke.

And I believed him. Mercy! Mercy! If A's were given for the dumbest, I would have been the valedictorian!

In that period of time, more than ever, I had wished for my grandmama. I needed her wisdom. So I turned to Mrs. Minnie, my mother-in-law.

Sitting on Mrs. Minnie screened-in porch that Friday evening around dusk, I enlightened her about those 2:00 a.m. phone calls from the same woman, asking for Luke. It had become such a nuisance that I called the operator to have some action taken. I was chattering on and on, when suddenly, Mrs. Minnie (who was known to speak her mind), mother instinct came forth. She blurted out, "What the *hell* do you mean, callin' the operator?" she snapped. "They will bring the F.B.I. in this, and you're gonna have all the Dunbars in the *damn* penitentiary!"

My jar dropped!

Finally speaking up for myself, my whiny voice trembled. "What do you mean Mrs. Minnie?" I asked. "How am I gonna cause that to happen?"

Mrs. Minnie stared at me with a cold hard look in her eyes. She said, "Georgann, you've got to learn to take some thangs in *this* life!" The movement of her lips stiffened, and her life experience emerged as her little hard-knot body bent over in her chair. She pointed her forefinger downward, "Gurl, as long as yo' asshole is facin' the ground, you gonna have problems!" Her forefinger then pointed straight out, and she said, "Only when yo' asshole is pointed this way, that you don't have problems in *this* life! So you had better learn to be *tough* in this world!"

Mrs. Minnie's words jolted me speechless.

At home, I cried my eyes out and wished for my grandmama...wished that I had listened to her...wished that I could go back in time.

Sobbing, I cried out, "Oh Mama, I need yo' help!"

I heard an inner voice speak to me, a voice that sounded like my grandmama's voice. "Georgann, get

up! Dry them tears and stop feelin' sorry for yo'self.
You have got to be strong!"

And strong I tried to become. But, did my
becoming a stronger person put my sons at risk of
growing up in a hostile environment? In an
environment where bad examples were displayed? In
an environment where their father should have been a
positive influence? In an environment where I became
the strict disciplinarian who was driven by fear of not
wanting to see my sons become another Dunbar
statistic? Looking back, I have often wondered, "What
if?" What if I had become a single parent? Perhaps
that could have made a difference in their future lives.
Who knows?

Chapter 11
Luke's no Role Model

That summer of 1977, at age eleven, Jeff accepted Jesus Christ as his Lord and Savior. I knew he was headed in the right direction, and that I was doing what the Bible says. "Train up a child in the way he should go, And when he is old, he will not depart from it," Proverbs 22:6. I felt that I was doing my job as a parent. Luke's nonexistence on weekends, public gambling, and our arguments were not going to affect our children.

In the month of September, on parents and teachers night, I was excited and ready to meet with Jeff's fifth-grade teachers. I walked into that classroom with a smile on my face, extended my hand and introduced myself to the black teacher, who looked to be in her thirties. Her hand dropped to her side. The smile quickly vanished from her face and she started busily rearranging papers on her desk. She spoke in a hostile tone. "Your son Jeff has become such a problem until I had to remove him from my classroom and put him in another!"

I felt as if I had gotten slapped in the face. I questioned, "Are you sure you're talking about *my* son?"

She swirled around, looked me directly in my eyes, raised her eyebrows and snapped, "Oh yes, your son, Jeff. He disrupts the classroom constantly!"

I was astounded--couldn't believe it! I thought, *Not my child! ... not Jeff!* He's the one that I can depend on when Luke hasn't shown up from his weekend escapades; those early Monday mornings when I go off to work, leaving Jeff in charge. He would handle himself like a little trooper. He made sure that Carl didn't play near the space heaters and that Carl got on the school bus. Jeff was too responsible of a kid to be acting out at school. *No, I* thought, *there has to be a mistake.*

But, in all honesty, I was apprehensive about Jeff's behavior even around the age of five. Jeff was a little carbon copy of Luke. Some even called him "Little Luke." He was a loving child, full of personality, he had an inquisitive mind, he was and not afraid of anything. But he was a strong-willed, hardheaded child. If I told him not to do something, I was just wasting my breath.

Probably, by most standards, Jeff's behavior was that of the typical boy. But reflecting back, I didn't look at Jeff as a typical boy. I looked at him as a Dunbar, and because I knew the history of the males in the Dunbar family. Most were high school dropouts, and had seen the inside of the penitentiary more than once. I was determined that wasn't going to happen to any child of mine. So, when he was disobedient, he was given corporal punishment; that didn't faze him. It became imperative that Jeff needed to be in church, 24/7! We attended Sunday school, morning worship, Wednesday night prayer meetings, and Jeff joined the youth choir. He attended Monday evening Bible study. But, as Jeff grew, his bad behavior in school grew as well. I considered it to be a miracle if a full month passed without getting a phone call from school. I thought, *Lord! I need some help with this boy!*

In desperation, I sought counseling for Jeff from our pastor, Reverend Townsel. He was invited to spend the weekend in their home. He also spent a week in camp on the Barksdale Air Force Base. I felt that sports built character, so Jeff joined the Sport for Boys Club. An avid sports enthusiast named Roy, who coached Little League teams, lived in the neighborhood and became Jeff's mentor in sports. Our desk became covered with Jeff's Little League sports trophies.

But Jeff was constantly in trouble at school and being suspended. He was either being disrespectful in the classroom, cutting class, or fighting. The more I disciplined, the more he rebelled. I prayed and read Bible scriptures with him. It had no positive effect on his behavior. I was at my wit's end. Luke was no help and set no example.

One evening, twelve-year-old Jeff came home from baseball practice, crying.

Alarmed I asked, "Jeff, what's the matter?"

"Mama, I'm tired of being teased about Daddy on that corner gambling!" The tears streamed down his face.

Comforting him in the only way I knew how, I looked him in his watery eyes and said, "Jeff, you're not responsible for what your father does. You just don't be like that!"

It was time to have another talk with Luke.

That night, I told Luke that a father is supposed to be an example for his son, and that his actions were causing some of Jeff's problems.

Luke looked blankly at me, as if I was speaking in a foreign language.

"What I do don't make Jeff act that way," said Luke. "I've seen children whose parents were alcoholics who made somethin' outta themselves."

On many occasions when I was informed of Jeff's behavior at school, I would get so angry and frustrated I responded with negative accusations by saying to him, "Boy what is yo' problem? Are you dumb, stupid, or just plain ignorant?"

I realize now, I was the ignorant one. Ignorant to the fact, that children mirror what they are exposed to.

I wanted Jeff to be this model child, when he was being shown the opposite of model behavior at home.

Chapter 12
Hypocrite! Hypocrite!

Luke's dirt hauling business wasn't going well. He wasn't making the payments on his pimpin' Lincoln car. My check was garnished and I was outraged! But Luke promised...he would do better. And surprisingly, he kept that promise, for a season.

Luke returned to what he knew best, working for a construction company. And for the longest time in years, Luke started handling his responsibilities consistently. Of course, he was still running those streets, but he was now prioritizing; putting family first. That year of 1977, Easter Sunday morning, Jeff, Carl, and Luke walked, but I strutted through the door at Morning Star Baptist Church with *my* family! I was as proud as a peacock, grinning from ear to ear...couldn't wipe that smile from my face!

In comparison to past years, that was a fairly "good" year. And I got too comfortable. And that's when all hell broke loose! Life afterward became a nightmare, but it wasn't Luke that wreaked havoc. It was ME!

It started in July of 1978: The construction businesses were booming. New subdivisions were going up in all areas of Shreveport, and the company that Luke worked for was in the middle of it all. Luke was bringing home a nice salary. Back in the day,

Western Electric was one of the best paying manufacturing jobs in our city. I felt very fortunate to be employed there. Our bills were few; being paid on time. For a change, the "Dunbar" household was relatively calm...too calm. And as that old saying goes, "the calm is just before the storm" surely applied to us.

With all the construction exploding in the city, I wanted to expand our home...like, monkey see, monkey do! So I dived in head-on, without reservations. I borrowed $5000 on a signature loan with my credit union, another loan with a finance company for the balance, and hired a contractor (who was too good to be true) without a signed contract. Six months later, after receiving his last payment, he walked away from the unfinished job...took the money and didn't return. I was frantic. We borrowed additional money from a bank, and hired another contractor who completed the work. That episode included two extra mortgages on our home within a nine-month period. Nevertheless, I was pleased with my large sized den, bathroom, closet and extended carport. But, it was as if the devil spoke, saying, "Let me throw a bomb up in there, and stir up some shit!" And that it did! All of a sudden, it was like, "BOOM!" and everything afterwards went haywire.

***

In 1979, Luke was fired. Our home was in foreclosure, and in the midst of it all, Luke came home one day without his big Lincoln car. He allegedly had a wreck in it, with it being towed off, but he was uninjured. I had my doubts because Luke, I noticed, was in a twilight zone of his own.

Luke, who never had a problem finding a job, suddenly wasn't interested in working. I sensed something was wrong with Luke, but I was too preoccupied with trying to straighten out the *mess* that I had gotten us into to give it much thought.

I thought things couldn't get any worse. I was wrong, for I had many miles to go, and many rocks to dig through before I would see a light at the end of *THIS* tunnel!

The plan was that Luke would drive me to work and pick me up, but if he couldn't make it there on time, he would call me so that I could make other arrangements. Throughout the week, the plans were being followed. But Friday came, and Luke didn't call and didn't show up. I had to hitchhike home and Luke came home about 12:30 that night.

"Luke, where have you been?" I yelled. "And how could you not come and pick me up when I'm allowin' you to use *my* car to find a job?"

Luke gave me an incognizant stare and suddenly blinked his eyes in recognition.

"Ann, I'm sorry!"

His speech was sluggish. I noticed the redness of his eyes and that dazed look. I hollered, "You've been smokin' that *mess,* and you are not using my car anymore!"

Luke slumped down into the chair, passed out.

Furiously, I tossed and turned all night. That morning I went to work, sleepless and stewing.

I had heard the old preacher say it many times, "The devil can show up, and show out!" But it had never fazed me, because I kept my head stuck in the Bible! Fact being, I was on a tightrope, trying to maintain balance...hold it together...not lose my sanity. So, I needed the "word." That's why I took it to work with me, and read it on my lunch breaks. How many times had I read, "Blessed are the peacemakers, For they shall be called the children of God?" But, I had always heard that "pressure can burst a pipe!" So, that Saturday morning, I was under pressure.

Working on Saturday's meant time and a-half pay. I needed that extra money. I tried to focus on that fact. But my mind was burning with anger at Luke and I brought that anger to work with me, instead of "the word." All my Bible readings and known scriptures were meaningless that Saturday. The devil had grabbed ahold on me and I was ready to show out!

I was in a ferocious mood, going about, doing my specific job as utility operator, (relieving my co-workers). I was wound up tight like a spool of thread, waiting to unravel. A feisty, reddish-blonde haired, green-eyed white co-worker said something to me. Any other time, I would have overlooked what was said, but, one word led to another. Then I heard *that* word.

Blinded by anger, I said, "No, she didn't call me a *bitch*?"

I could hear in the background a co-worker yelling, "Don't go 'round there!"

My long legs dashed around to the other side of the table where she sat. My hands grabbed her by her forearm in a vise-grip. I was in her face, through clenched teeth I said, "I am not here to be harassed by you or anyone else." My fingernails were digging into her forearm, as adrenaline fueled my anger. The more I talked to her, the deeper my nails pierced into her skin.

"Get outta my face, nigger!" she shouted.

My cheek felt the sting of her backhanded slap.

I lost it.

My fists were pounding, pounding, and pounding...using her head as a punching bag! The frustrations felt, because of my chaotic life, they were acted out by every blow of my fists ...This lick is for the loss of my home ... Pow! This lick is because of my frustration by Jeff's behavior in school ... Pow! And these licks are because I am frustrated, disgusted and furious with my husband, Luke ... Pow! Pow! Pow! ... I was taking all my pent-up fury out on that poor lady. *"Get her off of me! Get her off of me!"* She screamed.

Suddenly, a black co-worker grabbed my arms from behind in an arm-locked position. She shouted, "That's enough now! That's enough, before you hurt her!" Everything happened so fast, it didn't seem real. We were both suspended without pay until further notice.

"Ooh Shit!" I cried, *"What have I done? Oh God! I'm so sorry! I shoulda stayed my* **ghetto-ass** *at home! I was trying to make that time and a half pay! ... Now I'm not gonna have* **any** *pay!"* I was devastated, humiliated, embarrassed and worst of all, I felt like a hypocrite!

I don't know how I managed to drive, boohooing; I was a cryin' sistah! ...big elephant tears were popping out of my eyes. I thought, *Please Lord! Let this be a nightmare!* The company had a very strict policy about fighting on its premises, and employees were usually fired on the spot. I knew my *butt* was in the frying pan, and I was going to be *fired*!

I had faced adversities in the past, but never so many at the same time. I'd already lost the house, and we were living in it as renters, Luke didn't have a job and now I had lost mine. It was unreal! The only thing I had left was my faith in God. I knew that I had done wrong and I asked for forgiveness.

Within that same week, Jeff, who was fourteen years old and in the eighth grade was also suspended for fighting...again! I thought, *Ahh, Lordy! How much more!* Ephesians 6:16, "above all, taking the shield of faith with which you will be able to quench all the fiery darts of the wicked one." Seemingly, those fiery darts were hitting me right, left, front and back. I was surviving only on faith, hope and prayers.

After Jeff's three days suspension, we, as a family, sat in the school administration office. "Mrs. Dunbar," said the assistant principal, "I can see that Jeff is an intelligent person. He comes to school well groomed. He has good manners. I can tell he has been taught well, but he will promise you stars and give you nothing!"

I looked at this white man and I saw in his eyes how disappointed he was with Jeff, because he had given him every opportunity to straighten up his act. Yet no matter how many opportunities Jeff was given, he would continue causing problems in school.

The representative from the School Board had a slew of grievances against Jeff. After she finished reading them, her recommendation was that Jeff be placed in the alternative program. Jeff was a "bad apple", and they couldn't have one bad apple spoiling the whole bunch.

I felt a knife piercing my heart as this white woman called my black child a "bad apple." And I didn't have words to come to his defense. I was so distressed by it all, I thought, *Lord! Jesus! ... Have Mercy*! I knew the issue wasn't about race. It was all about Jeff's behavior.

My spirit was sinking to its lowest. I felt I had lost a cherished friendship with my white friend and co-worker, Ann. But going into my second week of suspension I had some visitors. Ann along with Debbie and Rita, both white, showed up at my door with four big bags of groceries. I was speechless.

Sobbing, I said, "I'm so sorry!"

It is a rare moment when Ann misses the opportunity to say something comical. However, with tears rolling down her cheeks she said, "Don't cry. We know you're a good person." We were all in tears standing in the middle of my kitchen. They gathered me in their arms and embraced me with love. In the midst of the dark clouds that hovered over my head, I was made aware that there is always a ray of sunlight in those clouds and at the right time it will appear. My three friends were that ray of light for me.

The next day my union representative called to inform me about the impending decision. She also informed me that one of my former supervisors, Winnie, (who had been promoted to a Department Chief) and another co-worker named Kathy, both white, had come forth and spoken in my behalf. I was humbly grateful. Then, the next day I was reinstated.

Oh, Praise the Lord! Thank you Jesus! I knew it was God's mercy, love and forgiveness of me that softened the hearts of those making the decision that allowed me another chance. After a two week suspension, I was happily back to work. A heavy cross was lifted off my shoulders. I realized I had brought the crisis upon myself.

***

Words couldn't have expressed my thankfulness for the *Civil Rights Act* of 1964. Martin Luther King Jr., and all those brave activists nationally and locally, who had fought for equality for Black folks. If it had been the 50's and early 60's, D'Artois and his posse would have arrested and billy-clubbed me, and locked my *black ass* up and thrown away the key...for beatin' up on that *white woman!*

But, two years earlier, on June 11, 1977, George W. D'Artois, whom *many* white folks once hailed as their "conquering hero," at age 51, had gone to meet his Maker. In D'Artois's glory days, his authority superseded Shreveport's mayors. However, D'Artois didn't go out with a blaze of glory. He made headlines in the daily papers for being a corrupt Commissioner. His *sidekick* Mooretown homeboy, Detective Leemon Brown, tried to keep from going down with the sinking ship...snitched on the Commissioner! ...*He took diarrhea at the mouth!*

Chapter 13
A Chicken being Plucked

One Saturday afternoon, while lying across my bed, I was in a state of despair at the condition of my marriage. I cried out, "Oh God! Is this man ever going to change? Please show me what to do!" I drifted off to sleep, and I had a dream. Abruptly, I awoke very disturbed. I had to have an explanation, and I knew who could give it to me.

***

Aunt Ida Mae was my grandmama's only living sister; all the others had gone to be with the Lord. Sitting in my great-Aunt Ida Mae's kitchen that Saturday evening, I felt that Aunt Ida Mae (who sometimes thought she was a dream interpreter) could surely interpret my dream. I watched her proudly do her Christian duty, making the unleavened bread for Communion... a task she took very seriously. Her back was turned to me as she stood at her kitchen counter with her apron on, a scarf tied over her head, making sure no hair got into her obligation. Her hands were busy rolling out that sacred dough.

"Aint Ida," I said, "I had a dream earlier today, and I don't understand it."

She added more flour to the dough and continued rolling. "Well, what was it about?" she asked.

"I dreamed that Jeff, Carl, and I were traveling on one of the main streets in Shreveport, trying to get home. We came to a fork in the road and I asked directions. I was told to take the road I was on. But that road led up a hill, and I couldn't see over it, and I was afraid. So I turned around, went back, and took the long way home. Then I abruptly woke up."

There was a moment of silence from Aunt Ida. Then she asked, "What's Luke been up to, now?"

Reluctantly, I answered. "He's still unemployed, stayin' out all weekends and sometimes weeknights."

Aunt Ida Mae slowly wiped her hands off with her dishtowel. She turned and faced me. Her eyes studied me, as if she was trying to figure out a way to tell me what she had been longing to say, and if she held her tongue any longer, she would burst. The deliberating words slid from her lips. "Georgann, 'dat is the Lord showin' you to step out on faith cause He'll be wit' you!" said Aunt Ida, "You see dat *ol' boy* ain't gon' do right!"

"But Aint Ida," I said, "Luke wasn't in my dream!"

"Dat's right! He wasn't in yo' dream. It was just you and yo' two chilluns." She continued. "Didn't you say you asked God to show you what to do, before you fell asleep?"

"Yes Ma'am."

"Well, God's showin' you what to do. Caint you see you can do betta without Luke?" She looked at me in disgust, and said, "Gurl, where is yo' faith? What God gotta do to git you to understand? Come down here and *hit* you over the head?"

I said to myself, "Aint Ida, don't know what she's talkin' about! Anyway, she had never liked Luke!" Her advice fell on deaf ears. However, those "forks in the road" dreams frequently made their presence in my sleep, and I would always go back from whence I came because of fear.

April 1980. Life continued as usual. Luke left home that Monday, the week of the Easter holiday. I could have had him on the missing person's list by Good Friday. That Saturday, my heart was heavy, but I cooked my Easter Sunday's dinner.

On Easter Sunday morning, the sun was shining bright and beautiful; a befitting day to represent the resurrection of Jesus. A day I decided to rise up out of bed and take Aunt Ida Mae's advice. I had had enough of Luke! I took some action.

Jeff, Carl, and I went to church. They were dressed in their new suits and shoes, and I was dressed in my new Easter outfit, as I prayed for strength. I didn't know what fate awaited me, but I really didn't think that Luke would give me too much of a problem. I had thought that any married man who is seldom home shouldn't have a problem leaving his "part-time" home permanently. But, man, was I wrong!

Easter Sunday's dinner consisted of roasted duck, cornbread stuffing, English peas, pound cake, two layer chocolate caramel filling cake, and sweet potato pie. But the only persons enjoying the meal were Jeff and Carl. As I sat at the kitchen table trying to digest my delicious dinner, a lump formed in my throat. I thought, *that old saying about the best way to a man's heart is through his stomach couldn't be true. Because Luke's heart and stomach were some place else! Not here! ...But who was he with? I know he can't be with another woman, 'cause Luke told me he wouldn't mess with any of those old "sluts" out there in them streets, when he got a woman like me to come home to. Yep! Brainwashed me! And I have always fallen for it.* Disgusted, I thought, *Daddy was right when he said that anybody that saw me walking down the street could tell I was a chicken, ripe for the pluckin!* Suddenly I had no appetite. I watched Jeff and Carl enjoy their meal.

As the evening got later, I couldn't ignore the growling of my stomach. I warmed the food that I had set aside earlier and again sat at the kitchen table and ate a small portion of the main course. Just as I anticipated having a slice of chocolate cake melting in my mouth, Luke walked in.

"Hey," he said.

"Hey."

"How you doing?"

Trying to act nonchalant, I answered, "I'm fine," and I continued eating my cake.

Luke went to the bedroom and he got a surprise! Not only was Luke surprised, I was also in for a surprise.

Luke made a flash back into the kitchen. I could feel the steam coming from his breath as he hovered over me. "What the *hell* you mean, packin' my clothes?" he yelled.

The chocolate cake suddenly tasted like hay. It made a big gulp as I swallowed it. Calmly I spoke, "I'm tired of you. I want you to get out of here, and you are going."

"Ain't nobody puttin' me out!" He shouted, "You go. You carry yo' motherfuckin' ass!"

My eyes bugged, and I caught my breath. Luke and I had been married sixteen years and he had never before used that type of language on me. I was literally stunned!

"You get outta here!" I yelled.

"*Bitch!*" he yelled. "Put me out!"

My heart dropped out of my chest. I had never seen Luke in such a rage. I was accustomed to Luke's apologetics; him saying, "Ann, I'm sorry. You're the *best wife* a man can have, and if I don't straighten up, I'm gonna lose you." But Luke had never seen me take action. Luke had grown accustomed to me thinking I was "commander and chief," when actually I was just as a "sounding brass or a tinkling cymbal"--- running my head, making a loud noise and never meaning anything. Luke was just as shocked with me taking actions, as I was shocked by his actions. Within seconds, Jeff and Carl entered the kitchen with a frightened look on their faces. Jeff cried out, "Mama what's wrong wit' Daddy? Why is he actin' like that?"

I shook my head, baffled by Luke's rage. I had actually thought Luke would make a peaceful exit from his part-time home. He continued yelling profanities and making threats. He was out of control. For the first time, I called the police on Luke... *he needed a knot snatched in his ass!* Luke cursed out the police! *Gone were the days of D'Artois's era!*

The police suggested that I pack a few clothes and leave until Luke calmed down.

The Big House, which once was a family haven wasn't there anymore. Most of the family had died. I had no money and no place to go.

Luke finally calmed down, packed his clothes, and he left.

I was free!

Three weeks later, the children and I were watching the 6 p.m. news on television. I heard the pain in Jeff's voice. "Look Mama!" said Jeff, "There's Daddy on T V in handcuffs!" The news reporter said "Two Negro males have been arrested for trying to run a scam on an undercover officer."

"Mama, why Daddy wanna do somethin' like that?"

"I don't know, Jeff. We'll just have to pray for yo' Daddy."

Eight-year-old Carl never showed any emotions.

Luke remained in jail several months before his unemployed brother paid the bond. However, before Luke could be released on probation, those papers had to be signed by a person with employment. And would you believe who signed the papers? Guess who! Reliable, tired of Luke, wanting to be free…Me!

Luke's employer not only hired him back, but was generous enough to allow him to bring home the company truck so he would have transportation to work. In 1 Corinthians 7:10-16 of the Bible, Apostle Paul wrote that the Lord commands the wife not to depart from her unsaved husband, because she may be able to save him. Therefore, being a self-righteous Christian…Luke got his "best wife" a man can have back! Now, how could he not change with all those blessings being bestowed upon him?

***

In July 1980, my hope was built on second chances. We got a second chance at our marriage, and after receiving our tax refund, we got a second chance at purchasing another home through owner finance. We moved into another section of the city. I had to get Luke out of Mooretown, so he could do better. But I soon learned, if the heart and mind of that person haven't changed, it doesn't matter where one lives. That first Friday of the following month, Luke left home that morning for work and did not return the entire weekend. I was devastated. I cried out, "Oh God, how many more opportunities must I give him? I am trying so hard to do what the Bible says, but it is getting so unbearable!"

My repetitive prayers for Luke to change were bouncing back off the ceiling. Every evening instead of coming home after work, Luke would stop in the old neighborhood and come home late at night, dazed and spaced out. His sleeping quarters were on the couch. The next morning he wore those same dirty clothes to work. His personal hygiene wasn't important any more, and there wasn't any more communication between us. I decided to let him be, but couldn't decide to let him go. Why, I didn't know.

***

In September of 1980, Jeff, now in the ninth grade, entered Fair Park High School. He seemed to be excited and enthused about making the football team. With his love for sports, I just knew things were looking up for Jeff. But it wasn't long before he would continue those same self-destructive behaviors; cutting class, tardiness, classroom disruptions, and suspensions. That next school year Jeff had to repeat the ninth grade. He was now a year behind his peers that he grew up with and played sports with. Wendell Davis, who later became a professional football player with the Chicago Bears, was one of those peers and Jeff's cousin. I sensed that Jeff was unhappy and I tried to get him to open up to me. But he refused.

***

On January 25, 1982 Jeff turned sixteen, and got an after-school job working part-time at a fast food restaurant within walking distance. Having a job seemed to have given him self-esteem, and he voluntarily gave me $20 every two weeks. I appreciated his contribution and was proud of him. If only he could have shown that kind of enthusiasm for school. It was as if he was deliberately being self-destructive. I was puzzled, confused, and frustrated by Jeff's actions, but I was constantly fighting for him to get that diploma. Looking back, perhaps Jeff's school life was a display and reflection on his dismal life at home. During that time, the only person seeming un-affected was nine-year-old Carl.

***

Summer! Thank God for Coach Roy, who worked diligently with the young boys in Mooretown. Although we were no longer a part of that community, Jeff remained a player on his team. Not only Jeff looked forward to those summer months, I basked in them. I could breathe a sigh of relief from those tense, frustrating, and aggravating nine months of school.

On the other hand, I wasn't given any outlet from Luke's behavior. He was giving me slowly simmering hell! It was as if the devil was out to get me any way it could. Although I was continually reading my Bible and praying, my marriage was on the down slope and I was getting more tense, bitter, and disillusioned. Luke had become a sinking ship, trying to hit bottom. And I wore my frustration, as my badge of honor, proof that I was a true Christian who longed to suffer and suffers long! Looking back, it doesn't seem real.

***

Two years passed and what I had thought would be a new beginning in a different part of the city had proven to be just a pipe dream. Before I realized it, April had arrived, and Easter was just around the corner. So was trouble. Luke, still hanging out after work, was arrested for assault on a police officer. Two months after his release from jail, Luke didn't have a job.

Once again, the pressure was on. Luke was out of work, the motor gave out in my car, and there was no extra money for repairs. I needed a cheaper house.

In September, we sold our home with the buyer assuming the notes, and back to Mooretown we went! With the down payment we received, I bought another car. Luke found a job with a construction company and his employer was a "Christian" Black man, along with many of his workers. One was a deacon, and Luke rode to work with him. Praise the Lord! This was the break I needed. Now Luke was definitely going to change! But, two weekends later, that Friday morning, Luke left for work and didn't return. The annoying, aching pain in my chest and left arm made it difficult for me as I packed his clothes.

Monday evening around five o'clock, Luke showed up.

Luke said, "Ann, I'm sorry. I had to ride from work with another man. We had a few drinks, then we went to this place where they were gamblin' and I lost all the money!"

Sighing wearily, I said, "Luke, you're getting worse. You have almost destroyed all the love I once had for you. If you keep doing me this way, there isn't going to be any love left!"

Luke said, "I know that you're the *best wife* a man could have, and if I don't straighten up, I'm gonna lose you." Luke pleaded, "Ann, please give me another chance. I promise you this won't happen again!"

Luke used those two words, "best wife" to psyche me. So, I unpacked his clothes. The irony of it all was I knew in my heart that Luke was lying, and that I would be played like a yo-yo; up one week and down the next.

However, I didn't want Luke to leave. Whenever I felt betrayed and hurt, I wanted him to go, but in reality I was only fooling myself. It was as if I was handcuffed to Luke. And when given the key to unlock the cuffs, I wasn't ready. Not yet! I still wanted to hold on.

Chapter 14
The Enemy Within

The house we now occupied was similar to our marriage ... in need of much repair! Within the two months we were there, my pastor, Reverend Townsel resigned and went to another church out of our parish. He made a visit to our residence and with his compassionate heart he offered us his home in an area adjacent to Mooretown called Hollywood Heights. It was for the same monthly rent that we were paying.

***

We settled into our "blessed home" the week before Christmas of 1982. For the first time since 1979 I felt content. I even had the audacity to be happy: Why not? We lived in a nice house, and Reverend Townsel was our landlord. His monthly visits, with a little informal counseling, could really help Luke. Along with Luke's co-workers and supervisor, he was about to get *Jesus* preached into him, and Luke was going to change. Holy, upon holy! I felt reinvigorated!

To my great expectations, some of his co-workers visited and had Bible study and prayers with Luke. I was thrilled. Our marriage was going to get better. There had to be some blood in this turnip!

After the Christmas holidays, Jeff, now in the tenth grade, transferred to a school within our district called Huntington High. He no longer had his after school part-time job, but that was my least concern. My major concern was that Jeff got an education and a diploma. Again I had great expectations of the change to a different school. I just knew that Jeff's attitude and behavior were going to improve.

***

On the 25th of January in 1983, Jeff turned seventeen. He had enrolled in ROTC and became squad leader of his class. To my delight, Jeff was definitely on the right track now. There would be an improvement in his grades, attitude and behavior. No more suspensions!

Within two months, Jeff was suspended.

After his three days' suspension was over, Jeff and I met with each of his teachers individually, and we were given a fairly decent report of his behavior, with the exception of one. She was a very young white teacher and in her first year of teaching. Her intense dislike for Jeff was clearly shown, as was Jeff's for her.

A very high-strung and emotional Jeff said, "Mama, she doesn't like me because I'm black!"

She replied, "No, I don't like you! But it's not because you are black. It is because of your behavior in my classroom. You are constantly disrupting my class."

They glared at each other fiercely.

I sympathized with Jeff's teacher. I knew first hand how frustrating Jeff's attitude could be. I loved my son and would have given my life for him, but I didn't like his behavior.

Jeff and I were left alone. I had reached my last straw with him, and pulled out the belt from my purse.

Jeff's eyes bucked, "Mama, what you fixin' to do?" he asked.

"I'm going to whip your ass," I answered calmly.

"You can't whip me in here!"

"And who's to stop me?" I showed no mercy.

Afterwards, I left him crying, and consoled by the school counselor. Being his mother, it never occurred to me that my actions had become an embarrassment to him. That he was embarrassed and tired of all the fussing and cursing that we, his parents, displayed before him. No, unfortunately that had not yet entered my unopened mind.***

It was summer of 1983, and soon-to-be twelve year-old Carl, who had grown by leaps and bounds, became a Christian and joined the Junior Usher Board. I was so proud of him. Carl's personality was the opposite of Jeff's. He was quiet and shy. When school began, Carl enrolled in Bethune Middle School, was in the sixth grade and doing well as always. With that sweet personality of his, I knew he would never have a behavior problem.

Luke, however, was another story. My ordeals with him had only scratched the surface. The house that I first thought would be a blessing seemed to have become infested with demonic inhabitants, doing evil acts. Seemingly that devil wanted to let me know who was in control, and it sure wasn't me. Luke's behavior and our confrontations were about to become more intense, fierce, and verbally abusive.

In the course of time, I finally came to the conclusion, that no matter what I did, and others who tried to help Luke, he was not going to change. However, if we were going to share the same residence, he was definitely going to make a financial contribution to the household expenses.

***

Luke had not been home since Friday morning. That Sunday night, my ears were sharp and alert, when I heard Luke's key unlocking the kitchen door. I stood there like a sergeant at arms, unaware that I was mirroring my grandmama, and those confrontations that she and my daddy would have. Only Daddy had never used the type of language to his mother that Luke was about to use on me, nor the lie.

I stared Luke down fiercely. My voice was calm and cold. "Luke, do you have any money to help with these bills?" I asked.

Luke's bloodshot eyes gave me an angry, piercing stare back.

"Gurl," you askin' me about money, and my brother is in Dallas 'bout to lose a arm and a leg!" said Luke.

"I can care less about yo' brother," I said, "my concern is about these *bills*!"

"Bitch!" Luke yelled, "You betta get the *fuck* outta my face!"

"I'm so tired of you! You get the *hell* outta here!" I shouted out, hysterically.

"Ain't no *motherfucka* gonna put me out of here! If anybody go, you'll go! You carry yo' motherfuckin' ass!" Luke yelled.

We were standing there in the middle of the kitchen floor glaring at each other like two fierce enemies. I remembered as a child what my grandmama had said, "Don't ever let a man think that you are afraid of him; if so, he would make mince-meat out of you!" So I felt that some protection was needed and I grabbed the first weapon I saw.

Suddenly, Jeff and Carl emerged into hostile territory and witnessed their mother with a butcher knife in her hand - and not for the purpose of cutting up parts of a chicken!

Luke had grabbed a chair and started toward me, yelling, "Bitch, you gonna cut me?"

"Yes!" I shouted, "I hate you!"

Suddenly, Jeff jumped between us. He grabbed my arm and cried out, "Mama, you see something is wrong wit' Daddy. He is acting crazy. Just leave him alone!" pleaded Jeff.

Luke and I both surrendered our weapons as Carl silently looked on. However, Luke continued ranting and raving, pacing back and forth and uttering vulgarities. For the second time in our marriage, I called the police. One of the Black officers who knew Luke, glared at me like I was a villain, a traitor. He took Luke into another room, and talked with him privately. Luke calmed down and they left.

Afterward, Jeff said, "Mama, I'm so tired of you and daddy arguin' all the time! I am just *tired* of it!" Tears streamed down his face.

"Jeff, I'm tired of it too!" I said. "But I'm not going to allow your father to do me any kind of way and not say anything about it!"

"Well, Mama you see it don't do you no good to say anything. All it does is start an argument!" said Jeff.

I looked at Jeff with tears in my eyes, realizing what he said was true.

Luke remained in the living room, sitting in the dark. Jeff, Carl and I went quietly to our separate rooms. I suddenly became aware of that annoying ache in my left arm and chest as I thought about what Jeff had said. That image of agony and frustration on his face continued to haunt me as I tried unsuccessfully to sleep.

Monday morning, all alone, I knew it was time for a lawyer. But I didn't have any lawyer fee. That wasn't going to deter me. After thumbing through the yellow pages, I came upon one that was offering what I needed...free consultation that same day. Oh thank the Lord! I knew my problems with Luke were about to be taken care of. This burden was finally going to be a thing of the past!

Three hours later, I was in more despair than I had felt previously. I was informed that Luke and I needed to be separated for several days before I could even file for a legal separation. I was given no light and felt that I was in a dungeon with no way out. I was finally ready to unlock those handcuffs, but I had lost the key. In reality, the key was in sight. I had it, with Luke's full cooperation. Those days he would be away from home...it was easy. So, why did I feel that the situation was hopeless? I guess I had been in the dungeon for so long, I was afraid to come out.

Anyway, I went back to my cell to complete my sentence, but it was with a hostile, silent fight.

I started doing anything and everything, trying to control Luke's behavior. If Luke didn't give me any financial support, he was not going to eat the food that I bought, nor was I going to wash his clothes. I would not confront him, but ignore him for that week, and maybe he would do better the next week. But taking those actions, played on my conscience, especially, trying to eat in his presence and knowing that he was hungry. In the final analysis, Luke would eat the food. I would roll my eyes, and murmur under my breath, "This nigga didn't bring his money home, and now he is eatin' the food that I bought with my hard earned money." I murmured, *"This nigga got his nerve!"*

In reality, my life had become precariously controlled, especially on Fridays, by the whims of Luke's behavior. As a result of this, I became an empty shell walking around ready to crumble at any given moment. I shall never forget that Saturday morning when I got spooked by a can of biscuits.

Actually, it all started Friday evening, when that 3:30 p.m. whistle blew; my first stop was the bank to cash my check, then off to the market. I hurriedly filled my basket with meats, fruits and vegetables. But my mind was, as always, filled with anxiety … hoping and praying Luke came home with money to help with his responsibilities. Well, Luke was a no-show, and that Friday night lying in bed, my thoughts were in turmoil as my mind went back, six months earlier:

It didn't take much persuasion, getting me to sign my name on the dotted line at that furniture store. The beautiful mahogany dinette table and six chairs stole my attention, also the soft brown leather sofa and recliner. I was reluctant, knowing we already had more than enough bills to pay. And I never knew from one week to the next, would the responsible Luke come home from work on Fridays, or would the irresponsible Luke be a no-show. Common sense was in the back of my head with a warning. "Girl, you know you can't depend on Luke!" But my eyes gleamed as I visualized replacing that nineteen-year-old antiquated aqua blue and white steel dinette set, and the old black leather sofa with the springs bursting out. Yes, we were in need of new furniture, badly. The entire purchase was a little over $3,000. However, Luke had promised me that I wouldn't have anything to worry about. He would definitely pay the monthly notes. Luke had not kept his promise. He had only paid one note. The entire situation flashed before my eyes.

Of course, I wanted to blame it all on Luke, but my conscience became a "whipping post" for past mistakes. My mind went back to 1979 when we lost our home because I didn't have enough patience.

Mama had always told me, "Georgann, you got to have patience. A baby hafta learn to crawl 'fore it can walk!" But crawling was never my thing! I wanted to walk and walk fast, and that's what had always gotten me in trouble. Now I was crawling, and scraping every penny to make the furniture payments.

So, that Saturday morning started out like far too many other Saturday mornings; I was in my "poor Georgann" mode. My chest felt tight, and I was filled with anxiety, but I dragged myself into the kitchen and started cooking breakfast. The pot of grits was slowly cooking as I put strips of bacon in the skillet for frying and got the can of Hungry Jack biscuits out of the refrigerator. And the oddest thing happened … my hands froze when I started to pop open the can of biscuits. I panicked …I actually became terrified. I thought, *Lord! What is happening? Why can't I pop open this can of biscuits? I've been preparing this same breakfast nearly every Saturday. And on weekend mornings experiencing these same feelings of having been tricked and betrayed by Luke, more times than I could count. So, what's up with the biscuit can?* My mind struggled to grasp what had happened. Perhaps it had been a figment of my imagination. Maybe I'm still asleep and having one of my crazy dreams.

I pinched the skin on my arm and felt the pain. "No!" I said aloud, "this is no dream. This is real!" I had a self-talk. "You're not going to get the best of me. I'm going to conquer this problem. I am not going to be outdone." Again, I placed my hands on the can several times, but my hands, heart and body just froze. The harmless can of biscuits could well have been a snake that had me frozen in my tracks, afraid to move! It was the most absurd scene one could imagine. It would have been comical, had I not been so frightened. After numerous attempts and frozen tense moments, I finally gave in to fear. Jeff couldn't understand why I had to have him come and open a simple can of biscuits. But neither could I!

I did my Saturday morning chores routinely. By 11:30, everything was done. Jeff and Carl went to the park to play basketball, and I was left alone in my abyss of despair. As I sat in my nice brown leather recliner, I thought about all the lies that I had tolerated from Luke. How hard I had worked to make ends meet while he made promise after promise after promise. And very seldom were they fulfilled. I said aloud, "Lord, I'm so tired of him! I'm just tired!" My voice faded in the distance. When I came to myself, I was sobbing hysterically, as if someone had died. I tried to contain myself, but the worse I became. I sobbed and shook uncontrollably. I cried out, "Oh Lord, help me! Please help me!" After not being relieved instantly, I thought, *I must get to the hospital and admit myself!* But realized I was in no condition to drive.

I cried out, "Oh Lord, help me to call someone to take me to the hospital." My mind scattered ... *who can I call?*

Something shouted out clearly in my mind, saying, "Call Reverend Townsel!"

I dialed the number. On the third ring ... Praise the Lord! Reverend Townsel!

Sobbing and shaking, I said, "Reverend Townsel... this is Georgann!"

"My dear, what is the matter?" he asked.

"I need someone to take me to the hospital."

"Take you to the hospital. Why do you need to go to the hospital?"

"Reverend Townsel, I'm so tired. I can't go on like this. I'm tired of trying to do the right thing, and Luke won't do right!" Still sobbing, I repeated. "I just cannot go on! No matter what I do, Luke won't do right!"

Reverend Townsel said urgently, "My dear, just hold on and let me pray for you, right now. You don't need to go to no hospital! Just hold on."

He prayed for me over the telephone, asking the Lord to calm the storm that was raging within me and had my mind so disturbed. I could feel the tranquility flow into my mind and relieve me of that distressful turbulence that had possessed me moments earlier.

***

Sunday morning I could hardly get out of bed, but I felt I must go to church. It was my only refuge; being with my church family and hearing the word of God. But, that Sunday morning, I sat on those pews with a dejected spirit, questioning God, "Why me? What have I done in my life to deserve this? Am I supposed to remain in this situation the rest of my life?" I had myself a pity party.

Reverend Townsel came by the following Monday evening, hoping to give counseling to Luke and me. But Luke still had not been home since Friday morning.

"Reverend Townsel," I asked. "Am I supposed to continue in this situation? I am *so* tired."

The preaching man of God, stared at me through his glasses, and looked puzzled. "My dear," said Reverend Townsel, "I *just* don't know. But read Psalms 37, Isaiah 40:28-31 and Job."

Perplexed and alarmed, I thought, *Lord! Am I going to have to be like Job?*

Before he left, the well-meaning Reverend Townsel, thought that he was giving me words of encouragement. He said reassuringly, "Hold on, my dear, God has not forgotten you. Just do the *best* you can and you are going to get your reward."

"*Reward!*" I screamed inwardly. "*Lord, when*?"

I thought about one of the old deacons who ended his devotional prayer, "Lawd! When I git to Heave', I wanna hear You say, Come on *up* thou good and faithful servant and receive yo' reward, you've been faithful over a few thangs. Now, I will make you ruler over *many*!"

I grunted, "Huh? I want my reward now! Because by the time I get to Heaven, I will have become too bitter and disillusioned to enjoy any reward!"

Luke showed up Monday night penniless as usual and looking like he had been on some sort of weekend binge. After my frightening experience, I felt that I was fighting for my life and had no energy or desire for accusations and arguments. Tuesday morning, at the breakfast table of pancakes and sausages (no can biscuits!), Luke looked guilty. I looked angry. Jeff and Carl just looked. No one said anything. I went to work seized by anxiety. *But, things will be better this week. Luke will surely bring the money home this week!*

***

Friday, I rushed home and sat in my recliner, stomach in knots, tense, and watching the clock … waiting for Luke like a warden … and thinking like a prostitute. *If Luke brings his money home, he just might get to warm my bed. But if he don't, he better sleep on that couch and better not try coming to my bed to touch me!* About five-thirty Luke came through the door. My tense body relaxed as I let out a heavy sigh and said, "Thank you, God!"

After my uncommonly restful and peaceful night's sleep, early the next morning I looked over at Luke lying beside me, still asleep. *Lord, why can't it always be like this? Why Luke have to mess up our marriage?* I said in a distressful voice, "Oh well. It is what it is."

That Saturday morning, in the kitchen I got spooked, again! I started to pop open the can of biscuits and I froze. I said, "Lord! What is wrong with me? This can't be real!" However, I tried, tried, and tried, but the thought of that biscuit can, making that pop opening noise was just too frightening for me.

I tried to rationalize why. Was it because on weekends, everything on the surface looked quiet and peaceful, but the reality was that seventy-five percent of the time, my mind was in turmoil? I was always tense and nervous, wondering if Luke was coming home on Friday's, and the loud, shouting arguments if he didn't have any money when he did come home. And Jeff and Carl's reactions … Lord, what were their reactions? Did they see the misery on my face? So they went about quietly, walking on eggshells. I didn't know. But, whatever the reason, opening a can of biscuits became a paralyzing, horrific hurdle that I never overcame.

Chapter 15
A Dream--Denied

My greatest desire for Jeff, other than having Jesus Christ in his heart, was that he would graduate from high school and live a productive life. So far, that had been an accomplishment seemingly impossible for a male Dunbar. It was very common for a male Dunbar to be a school dropout, in jail, going to jail, or getting out of jail. Carl and Jeff were not going to go down that path, not if I could prevent it. I was not going to become another "mother of a Dunbar" who visits her sons in the jailhouse. No way! My sons were going to make something of themselves other than a life of crime.

Jeff, who had the ability to do well academically, would not apply himself. Although his report card had shown failing grades, I was determined that he was going to remain in school until he received that diploma, however long it took. That was my desire for Jeff. And I had thought that I would not accept anything less.

***

Spring came and our household, for a change, was relatively quiet. Jeff, who was a very good athlete, was on the school's baseball team. His coach was very impressed with his pitching skills and proclaimed that

Jeff could become eligible for a baseball scholarship to college, providing he continued in school, and improved his grades. How excited I got! My son going to college...that was a dream that I never dared to have. I would have felt that I had won the lottery if he just finished high school! However, Jeff was not disciplined. When he should have been at baseball practice, he would do the opposite—hang out in the gym, playing basketball. After his coach and I talked with him, he seemed to settle down. And I was so looking forward to going to his school games and cheering him on.

One Monday evening in April, Jeff informed me that the baseball team had an upcoming out-of-town game Saturday, but they were going to leave from school that Friday morning and return home Saturday evening.

I was so delighted that he was finally accomplishing something positive that I didn't question him and gave him extra money for the trip.

That Saturday morning the telephone rang. To my surprise it was a recorded message from the school saying Jeff did not show up for school Friday morning.

I became very worried. But, Luke didn't get alarmed. He said, "That boy just lied and wanted to stay out all night away from home."

"If that's the case then he will be punished!" I said angrily. "And if he's not here by tonight I am going to call the police and report him missing."

All day Saturday I anxiously waited for Jeff. Saturday evening around six o'clock he finally came home.

"Jeff, where have you been all night?"

"I've been out of town with the baseball team."

"No you haven't." I snapped, "I received a message from your school this morning, saying you did not show up for school yesterday!"

His eyes bucked, realizing he was caught in a lie; he said, "I stayed all night with a friend."

I said, "Since you have lied to me, you are not to go to the prom next weekend."

Jeff came unglued. His eyes had an "I hate you look" in them. He burst out in anger, "If I can't go to the prom, then I don't want to go to school any more!"

"Oh, yes! You are going to school if you stay in *this* house!" I commanded. "But you are not going to the prom!"

"Well Mama," he said in defiance, "I just won't live here any more!"

"Where are you going to live?"

"I don't know, but I just can't live *here* any more!"

Luke, who had remained silent, said, "Let him go. If that's what he wanna do, then let him." He continued with a warning. "He will find out it ain't as easy out there as he thinks it is!"

"Son, do you know what you're doing?" I asked.

Jeff looked at me with tears in his eyes and said, "I don't know, but I know that I can't live here with *you* any more!"

"Jeff," I said, "you're seventeen years old and if you don't want to be here, then I can't force you to live here!"

He went into his room, packed his clothes and walked out the door with his suitcase.

My heart felt shattered. An overwhelming feeling of defeat suddenly washed over me. I went into my bedroom, closed the door, and wept. I cried out, "Oh God, what have I done that's so wrong?"

I spent that night in torment, questioning why everything I had done thus far had failed. My marriage, my son, everything! The only logical explanation was that God was punishing me. This was my punishment for disobeying my grandmother and marrying Luke.

I sobbed, "Oh Mama, I am so sorry for disobeying you! Please forgive me!" Then I prayed asking for forgiveness from God.

Jeff had been away for three days. That Tuesday night around seven o'clock, there was a knock at the door. Jeff was escorted by my neighbor. She said that he wanted to talk with me and she left.

Jeff said, "Mama, I'm sorry for the way that I acted, and I want to come back home."

I let out a sigh of relief, as that heavy burden was lifted off my chest and I gladly accepted my wayward son back into the fold, even if it was shabby. He was my son…and I was his mother!

Jeff said, "Mama, I don't want to go back to school."

"No way!" I said, "You're going back to school."

"Mama, I don't want to go to school any more. I want to get a job, and go to barbering school."

"You can't go to barber school without a high school diploma."

"I can get my GED while going to school for barbering." Jeff said.

I gave Jeff all the rebuttals against him dropping out of school. Luke tried talking Jeff out of his decision. Neither of us was successful. Jeff's mind was definitely made up to quit school.

I suddenly remembered Jeff's continuous problems in school, and from the evidence of his last report card, he was going to repeat the tenth grade, again. He just seemed not to care. I felt defeated and a failure as I reluctantly gave in to him. But, not without his assurance, that he would definitely go to barber school as soon as he found a job. Jeff made me a promise, gave me his word.

That next morning Jeff dropped me off at work, and he went job hunting. Within two weeks he had a job. Two months later he was fired.

In November of that same year, after having worked on several jobs and not keeping them very long, Jeff, at the tender age of seventeen moved to Dallas, Texas to live with a friend.

***

January 25th of 1984, Jeff wasn't home to celebrate his eighteenth birthday. Life seemed so strange without him around, but I was gradually accepting his departure. As much as I regretted his dropping out of school and leaving home, it was somewhat of a relief not to have to be stressed by those turbulent school seasons with Jeff. I looked forward to finally not having to be bombarded with calls from his school, on my job and at home. But, there seemed to be no rest for the weary!

***

In March of that same year, Jeff was unable to decide where he wanted to live. He had come back home to live once, then returned to Dallas and at my expense, and was home again.

But just as I felt relieved of Jeff's emotional roller-coaster events from school...I was blindsided! Carl who was in the eighth grade and never any problem, suddenly got suspended! He had been disrespectful to his teacher.

Carl had expressed displeasure at being placed in the physical education class being taught by a female coach. She had precisely asked for Carl because of his good behavior. However, he made it known to her in very disrespectful words that he wasn't pleased with that decision.

I was totally surprised by Carl's behavior. I knew that I had better take some drastic action before he too, got out of hand. I was definitely not going to go through that same course of events with Carl that I had with Jeff. After Carl's three days of suspension were over, I took him back to school and brought a "friend" along also. The school counselor granted me permission to use her office and I pulled out of my purse my friend, the belt.

Afterward, I accompanied Carl to his class and we both offered an apology to his teacher. Carl had gotten the point; behavior problems would not be tolerated from him. Little did I know my troubles with Carl had just begun!

Chapter 16
The Butt Whuppin'

That same year produced the undeniable evidence that my marriage was at its worst. Luke and I had been married twenty years, and as volatile as our relationship had gotten, he had not physically abused me. The handwriting was on the wall, but my head was held so up high that I never looked down to read the sign. Because of my snobbish attitude: no money, no accommodations. Luke had had enough of my highfalutin' ways, and was going to show me how to control a bossy wife and put her in her place.

Luke felt his oats that Friday evening; He came home, handled up on his financial responsibilities, so he felt entitled...

"Georgann, let me use yo' car. I'll bring it back tonight," said Luke.

"No, you can't use my car," I answered, "because you used it last Friday and brought it back Saturday morning with a big dent in it, and acted as if nothing happened."

Luke's eyes narrowed. He stood over me and snapped, "You Western Electric women jus' think y'all so *high* and *mighty*."

Smoke came from my nose. I gave him a tongue-lashing. "When you don't bring home any money, *this* Western Electric woman keeps this house afloat. Cause I sho' can't depend on you! I pays the bills, and put food on the table while yo' stupid, dumb-ass throw yo' money away!"

Luke eyes turned fiery red. He shook his fist in my face saying, "You need a good ass whuppin'. That's what you need!"

I was astonished. Luke's irate behavior was so sudden it caught me off guard. My heart began to race. I jumped off the bed and wandered foolishly into the bathroom, eyes looking wildly and randomly for something to defend myself with.

"What is the matter with you, Luke?"

"You just need a good *ass* whuppin'!"

I swirled around and glared Luke in his eyes. "You're not gonna give me one!"

"Oh, Yeah!" said Luke.

Then I felt the blows of Luke's fists pounding on the top of my head like a ball bouncing off a bow-low bat …coming left and right; pop! whop!...singing a tune. And the name of that tune was "I'm Tired of You." *I'm tired of you insultin' my manhood! I'm tired of you callin' me dumb and stupid. I'm tired of you thinkin' you somethin' cause you work at Western Electric and makes mo' money than me. Well I'll show you, Miss High and Mighty! If I can't do nothin' else right... I betcha I can whup yo' ass right!*

Losing my balance, I fell between the bathtub and the commode. With determination and revenge, I somehow managed to get myself up from the floor. But his blows kept coming on the top of my head. With him right at my heels, I ran into the kitchen. And being a "ghetto, nappy-headed-sistah" I grabbed for the butcher knife.

"You son-of-a-bitch!" I yelled. *"I'll kill you!"*

Luke's eyes bucked, and he said daring, "Oh! You gonna cut me?"

Luke was swinging his hands wildly, hitting out and trying to take away the knife.

I lashed out at his hands and drew blood.

Luke yelled, *"Bitch, you cut me!"*

My feeling of rage turned to shock. The knife dropped out of my hand, and I started walking.

Yanked backward by my hair, I felt the cold sharp edge of that knife at my throat. "Bitch!" said Luke, "I ought to kill you!"

Time stood still.

I heard the throbbing of my heartbeat, but I didn't panic. I don't know whether it was the shock of disbelief at what just happened or what, because I was never one for bravery. But, since I was a saved, sanctified, and "on my way to Heaven anyhow

Christian," my voice spoke calmly. "I'm prepared to die, Luke."

OHMYGOSH! What was I thinking?!!

"This bitch done cut me, and I can't even hurt her!" Luke said in amazement.

He let go of me and I walked out of the house and started toward my car.

Luke appeared at the door with a hammer in his right hand, and the knife and a towel wrapped around the left one. He threw the hammer. It hit the lower part of my back. Numbed …I felt no pain. As quick as a cat, Luke ran out to the car and thrust the knife into the tire on the front driver's side. "Bitch!" said Luke, "you ain't goin' no where!"

The entire scene was surreal. It was as if I was watching a violent movie, as I stood watching Luke walk back into the house. I followed, in a daze, phoned Luke's sister and told her Luke needed to go to the hospital. Luke came out of the bathroom and left the house, walking. Suddenly Jeff came bursting in the house. "Mama!" he cried, "What happened?"

"Your Daddy attacked me and I cut him in his hand!"

"Daddy did what?"

"He hit me and I cut him."

"I'm gonna kill him!" Jeff shouted.

"No!" I said, "Let it be. It is over with!"

With tears streaming down his face, Jeff said, "I got to get outta here!" and he ran out of the door.

I yelled, "Jeff wait!" without getting a response.

I stood there in a trance and thought, perhaps I am having one of my bad dreams and the blood is going to disappear. But the evidence was on my blouse and pants, and on the wall and the floor...Luke's blood.

I cried out, "Oh God! How did all this happen?"

Still in shock, I gathered enough strength and began to clean up the blood, when I heard a car pull up into the driveway. My cousin Mary was flabbergasted by all the blood that covered me. Glancing around the room, she said, "Georgann, Jeff came to the house very upset and said that Luke had attacked you. And he was gonna find Luke and kill him."

"Where is Jeff?" I asked in anguish.

"We finally got him calmed down, and I left Sonny talking to him."

I exhaled quietly.

Jeff was in good hands with Sonny, Mary's husband.

Mary and I cleaned until we removed all the blood. Before leaving, she said, "Georgann, this should be enough now. You have taken and taken. Enough is enough!"

"Mary, you're right. I've taken all I'm gonna take. This is it. I'm through!"

All alone, I suddenly remembered Carl, who was playing in the neighborhood. I thought, o*h God, I can't let him see me in this condition!* I threw my bloody clothes into the trash, and showered.

When Carl came home, everything appeared normal. But, I knew I had to explain the situation to my son.

"Carl," I said, "I've got something to tell you."

"What is it Mama?"

"Yo' Daddy and I had a fight. He attacked me and I cut him in his hand."

The tears that I tried so desperately to hold back begin spilling from my eyes. I continued, "I'm so sorry for hurtin' your Daddy!"

Twelve-year-old Carl didn't blink an eye. He looked at me and said very calmly, "Mama, the nigga was tryin' to hurt you, so you did what you had to do."

Stunned! I cried out within myself, "Oh God! What am I doing to my child?"

Carl went into his room, leaving me ashamed. I was ashamed of myself for allowing my marriage to become so out of control and all screwed up. I was ashamed that my life was in such chaos. I was ashamed of the example I put before Jeff and Carl and that I had subjected them to such a tumultuous life. I said within, "This fairy tale is definitely over. It is long past time for me to take these handcuffs off and be free!"

I arose at dawn with a purpose. Those empty cardboard boxes had been saved for just the right time. I began to pack Luke's clothes, with a deliberate motive. Then I heard the familiar sound of that key unlocking the door. I cried out in despair, "Oh Lord, please don't let that be Luke!" But, there he was, with his hand bandaged up.

I showed no compassion and I ordered him out.

Luke was like a wounded animal, staking his claim. With a determined look on his face, Luke said, "Gurl, you better leave me alone! Cause I'm gonna stay here until my hand is well, and I mean it!"

I suddenly felt guilt and remorse at what I had done to him. I thought this was the least I could do for him, since it was my fault he was in that condition. As a result of that incident, the ligaments on two of his fingers had been cut severely and surgery had to be performed. He was going to be out of work at least six weeks.

It was time to call for the Preacher!

I telephoned the new pastor of our church, Reverend Murphy Hunt. I felt that I had drained Reverend Townsel, so now it was Pastor Hunt's turn. What better way for him to get a personal invitation of introduction into the *Dunbar* family than by an act of violence. With our situation, I knew I would be calling on him...big time. If our family didn't drive him out of the ministry, he had to be sent by God!

***

Monday evening, around 5:30 p.m., the tall and stout framed, Reverend Hunt's presence filled the door as he stood in the entrance. He spoke with such a courteous tone. "Mr. Dunbar," he said, "your wife called and asked me to come and talk to the two of you. Will it be alright with you if I come in?"

A surprised Luke stood up and said eagerly, "Yes, Reverend Hunt, it's alright."

We sat in the living room and for the first time in two days, Luke and I spoke indirectly to each other.

"Reverend Hunt," I said, "the situation has gotten so bad here, this violence was inevitable." I gave him a rundown of what had happened that Friday night.

Reverend Hunt sat quietly, listening, as Luke gave him his version. Then out of the blue, Luke said, "Rev., I don't know what don' got into her lately. I guess she got another man, or somethin'!"

I looked at Luke and was dumbfounded. And beyond my wildest imagination, I couldn't have looked any more foolish. Even the Catholic confessors have dignity about themselves, but not this "Holier-than-thou" Baptist. I grabbed the Bible, put my right hand on it, and dropped to my knees, "Reverend Hunt, I swear, I don't have another man!"

The mild-mannered preacher man's, reddish complexioned face turned beet red. His mouth opened and his eyes stretched. The embarrassed Reverend Hunt said, "Get up off your knees, Sister Dunbar!"

It happened so spontaneously. I could only imagine what my pastor thought; His first counseling session with his faithful, Bible-carrying, scripture-quoting church member who had used a knife on her husband, and was now in my grandmama's words making a "sho' nuff" fool of herself by grabbing the Bible and swearing on it! He definitely had his work cut out for him with this Dunbar family...especially with this faithful member. Luke knew that he was an unsaved sinner. But I wasn't what I had thought I was... a bona fide, strong spirit-filled Christian. I was filled, but it certainly wasn't with the Holy Spirit.

Nevertheless, Reverend Hunt gave Luke and me our first counseling session at a very difficult time, putting special emphasis on violence in the home.

"Reverend Hunt," said Luke, "I promise you there won't be any more fightin' here and as soon as my hand gits well enough for me to go back to work, I will be leavin' here!"

I couldn't wait for that to happen. Just the thought of becoming a free woman in a couple of months made my heart do a tip-tap-toe dance! And my mind screamed a song, FREEDOM IS COMING! FREEDOM IS COMING!

Chapter 17
Full Blossomed Bitch

Six weeks dragged. Luke and I were being tolerant of each other. Actually, I felt it was an opportunity for me to redeem myself for my act of violence. I considered the fact that Luke could have killed me when he had the knife at my throat. I realized that in spite of all the conflicts and animosity between us, the core of Luke's heart was still soft. I was so thankful that Luke restrained himself. So, (not being intimate, nor kissing Luke's feet) from my guilty conscience, I submissively waited on him.

***

The six weeks ended, and Luke was working again, and knew just what it took to appease me—Money! 1Timothy 6:10, "For the love of money is the root of all evil:" I guess I was living proof of that! Because I couldn't have cared less whether Luke came or went. Just bring the MONEY home!

***

Several months had passed and Luke was faithfully "bringing in the bacon." Then it was April, 1985. Thank the Lord for income tax refunds. We could never make any major move without those income tax checks; we split the $800. Luke needed a car, and he had a scheme.

Luke, insisting that I come along for the ride, drove directly to this one particular car lot where he was supposedly seeing this specific car for the first time, a 1972 Cadillac. And no Cadillac money! The selling price was $1100. Looking at that Cadillac was a total waste of time, so I had thought. Luke left me outside while he went inside to talk with the manager. Fifteen minutes later Luke returned.

"I've made a deal with the manager," said Luke, "but he wants to talk to you too."

"Why he needs to talk with me?" I said, "I'm not having anything to do with this."

Luke said, "Ann, he just wants to ask you a few questions. That's all."

Suspiciously, I said, "Luke, you are not going to get me stuck with yo' car payment, because you and I both know that you are not going to pay your bill."

Luke declared that in all honesty, the manager just wanted to talk with me, and did not need me to co-sign for him.

With *"SUCKER"* stamped on my forehead, I reluctantly walked into that office and was conned. Before I realized it, my signature was on those papers, with a definite promise from the manager, that Luke would be solely responsible for those car payments, and I didn't have anything to worry about.

***

Two Fridays later, the real Luke didn't come home. He had returned to his weekend habits. After the third month of not receiving duns from the car company, while at work, a small inner voice spoke, "You need to call and check to see if Luke is paying his car notes." Without any hesitation, I immediately made the phone call.

The secretary said, "No, Mrs. Dunbar, your husband hasn't made a payment in three months and we have started garnishment procedures on you."

I was devastated, and knew that my job would be in jeopardy if the garnishment papers became official. The company had strict rules concerning garnishments and I already had two on my record from past experiences. But in those last three years, I had begun re-establishing my credit by making many sacrifices. Now, to have my job at risk was terrifying. I went into the restroom, torn up.

I finally got myself composed, went back to my work area, and prayed. "Thank you God, for placing that phone call on my mind! Now help me to get out of this situation. If not, I could lose my job! And this job is all I have to depend on!" I cried, "Please God! Help me!"

After work, face to face with the white manager, who sat upright behind his big desk and looked sharply in my face. "I'm sorry Mrs. Dunbar," he said, "but Luke's construction job is unreliable to garnish his wages. Yours is more reliable!"

I cried, "If you garnish my wages, I won't have a job!"

"Well, if you can give me the entire balance today, I won't send the paperwork in." said the manager.

Tears ran like a water faucet down my cheeks, desperately trying to figure out where I could borrow $345 that day. *My cousin Mary and her husband Sonny!* When I arrived at their home I was a complete mess…sobbing uncontrollable.

Sonny immediately wrote out a check to the finance company and I returned and paid the balance of Luke's car note. God bless Sonny and Mary. I couldn't thank them enough!

Luke agreed to pay the indebtedness with $50 weekly. He came home on Friday's and acted like a responsible man. And would you believe I began to be hopeful again? For the mere fact that another man had to straighten out his mess, I felt had brought some remorse and shame to him.

Yes! Luke definitely was changing!

***

For three months, I was afforded that luxury. However, after the debt was paid, Luke reverted to his old habits. Luke hadn't changed. But I had.

On those special first Sunday's of every month was Communion. I had always taken that bread and wine with a feeling of gratitude and thankfulness. I had thought that I had a pure heart. But that particular Sunday night the leftover fried chicken that Jeff, Carl, and I had feasted on earlier remained on the stove in a covered dish. About 7 p.m., in walked the absent husband and father from Friday morning. Seeing Luke brought resentment upon me so, until I actually loathed him.

Luke nodded.

I didn't acknowledge. I said to myself, "I called yo' Mama's house lookin' for you. She hadn't seen you. I had Jeff to go lookin' for you. He couldn't find you. So now here you come lookin' like some throw-a-way and I know you done gambled up all yo' money. Well I'm not speakin' to you!"

Luke's eyes wouldn't meet mine as he walked over to the stove and grabbed up a drumstick from the dish; his salivating mouth was ready to attack that drumstick like a hungry dog attacks a bone. I railed silently, *"I work all week, pay out all my money on bills and bought food and yo' black-ass work and throw yo' money away. Now here you come, wantin' to bite your chops into the meat that I spent my money on. Nigga, you make me sick!"*

I tried to restrain my feelings, but I had a raging storm inside of me and all my anger and resentment came forth when the drumstick was within inches from Luke's lips. Like a two-legged snarling bitch pit bull, I leaped toward Luke, snatched the drumstick out of his hand and threw it to the floor as hard as I could. That juicy-plump drumstick did a hop-skip-jump, and landed in the corner. In a cold-blooded and callous voice, I said, "You didn't bring yo' money home, so you don't eat *my* food!"

Luke was startled.

My hateful words were piercing, as I continued, "I'm sicka' you usin' me! If you work and don't bring yo' money home, you eat where you took yo' money. Cause you ain't eatin' anymore free food here! And I'm not washing yo' clothes either!"

Luke didn't give a rebuttal. He just walked past me with a hurt look on his face.

It never entered my mind that Luke could have beaten me to a pulp if he so desired. But I would have fought to the very end to keep him from sinking his teeth into that drumstick. I didn't care what the Bible says about feeding the hungry. Luke's hungry ass could have *starved* for all I cared!

***

That year, Jeff and I also were constantly at odds. He couldn't maintain a job for very long and I was always, as he phrased it, "on his case," which only caused more tension and distance between us. It seemed that the atmosphere in our house went from cool to cold and back. The only short-lived happy moments which I can recall were when an opportunity was offered for Jeff to have a great future:

I danced around the house in blissful joy. "Thank you Lord!" I cried, "My troubled son is getting another chance! Thank you! Thank you! Thank you!" Wednesday evening, I had intercepted *that* phone call. A coach from a local private college heard about Jeff's baseball skills. He offered to allow Jeff to get back into school and get his diploma. The coach said that he would personally see to it that Jeff received a baseball scholarship to that college. *What an opportunity for Jeff!* I just knew he would be as happy as I was. After the third call from the coach and Jeff never returned his calls, the coach never called again. Jeff could have cared less. *So much for my blissful joy!*

It wasn't long afterward that Jeff lost another job, and our ongoing arguments about not showing responsibility were on again.

A teary-eyed Jeff angrily said, "Mama, all you do is fuss at me. I get tired of hearing those same old words all the time."

"Jeff, I get tired of repeating myself to you. But the fact remains, if you are to stay here, you must work and keep a job," I fired back at him in anger.

"You have always gotten on my case about somethin'!" said Jeff. "Ever since I can remember, you were always calling me stupid or dumb and comparing me to my cousin, Wendell. Or, if you got mad at Daddy, you would take it out on me!" Jeff cried.

OUCH! …That really made an impact, and called for a reality check.

Guilt surfaced as I thought of the times I had yelled at Jeff and said things to him because of my frustrations and fears. I could not understand his attitude of not wanting to make his life better. I feared that if he didn't have a positive desire for his future, he would eventually lose direction and end up in trouble … just like those Dunbars!

Was I harder on Jeff because of my fears? Had I punished him for every little offense that he committed? Did I see the negative and never validate the positive in him? It seemed the more I tried to enforce my rules upon him, the more he rebelled and seemed to resent me. And the harder I tried to keep him from developing what I thought were those Dunbar characteristics, the more Jeff gravitated toward their ways.

But, wasn't that my job as a mother? To keep my son from going down those wrong paths. It was all left up to me. I had to control his behavior and save my son. If I didn't do it, who else would? Could I depend upon Luke?

Had I made a comparison of Jeff with Wendell, who had done well? I did recall one occasion. Had I gotten angry with Luke and taken it out on Jeff? Perhaps, unconsciously I had, but never intentionally.

I felt terrible, and said, "Jeff, I'm sorry I said those things to you. I was just trying to make you do better, and maybe I went about it the wrong way and I am sorry." I continued, "But, that doesn't give you an excuse to not keep a job and make your life better."

Jeff didn't respond.

That same week, Jeff secretly returned to Dallas. Not long afterward, he was arrested on a misdemeanor charge of unauthorized use of a movable, and was incarcerated. My worst fear for him had come into existence.

Chapter 18
No Bright Side

Being home on those rare Sunday morning's Luke would faithfully watch the Jimmy Swaggart Ministry on television. He would repeat the prayer that the minister gave, and his big crocodile tears would be just as many as the minister's.

Watching Luke's reactions to that program was like pulling for a race horse to win the Kentucky Derby. I would look over at Luke, and the tears would be running from his eyes. My heart would beat wildly with excitement and anticipation, as I silently prayed for Luke, "Lord, please save him! Please save him!" Knowing in that moment, he was going to fall to his knees, hands in the air and saying, "Oh Lord! Thank you Jesus, I'm saved!" But that didn't happen. Not in the way that I had thought it would be. Over the years, the prospects of Luke's changing had grown dismal. Fact being, I was unaware of the struggle that was going on inside of Luke…a war that he had no control over.

Nevertheless, Luke decided that he wanted to become a Christian. On that fourth Sunday morning in March of 1986 Luke, at the age of forty-two, was baptized. Evidences those calluses on my knees beseeching God on Luke's behalf had finally paid off. Now we were, equally yoked! That next Sunday,

Luke, Carl, and I attended church as a family. After that Sunday Luke never went back to church. And that was the end of that episode.

Although my happiness for Luke was short lived, I still had something to be thankful for. Jeff was released after seven months of incarceration. We drove to Dallas and brought him back home. My family was together again. Even if the conditions were shabby, I had thought things were going to get better.

But, on the contrary, my life that I considered the "pits" had only been treacherous thunderstorms. The real tornadoes were about to hit, and I would feel as if I had no shelter.

***

September 20th, 1986, Carl turned fifteen years old. He had quickly sprouted to be six feet tall and was still growing. He had been promoted to the ninth grade and would be attending Huntington High School. Carl's personality was changing as rapidly as he grew.

Now Carl was fighting in school, disrespecting his teachers, and failing in his subjects. He was going down that same path as Jeff had gone, but Carl's behavior was more aggressive than Jeff's. Seemingly, I was in a whirlwind that was going around and around, and would often ask, "Lord, will it ever come to an end?"

I was constantly giving lectures and demands, which were totally being ignored. Jeff, who was twenty years old, would not keep a job, or his 2 a.m. curfew. We were still locking horns. I was trying to have some rules, regulations, and order in a disorderly household.

It was during this period that Luke came home one Sunday morning without his Cadillac. I don't remember to this day what his reason was for not having it, because now my mind was totally perplexed with Carl's actions. While I was trying to comprehend it all, Carl was arrested.

One Saturday evening, at about 5 p.m., Carl asked permission to go to the video arcade at the mall. I regretfully had to deny him. Very seldom was there any extra money for those luxuries, because eighty-five percent of the time I carried the load of the household expenses.

Luke was actually home that Saturday and said, "Let the boy go to the mall with his friends. You can't keep him penned up in this house all the time."

Against my better judgment, and with apprehensions, I gave Carl my permission with him having a 9 p.m. curfew…without any money!

Approximately 10:30 p.m., I was anxious of his whereabouts. Ten minutes later, the phone rang. Carl was at juvenile station.

As we headed down the interstate, Luke apologized. "Ann, I'm sorry. You were right. Carl didn't need to go to the mall without any money."

We finally arrived at the station, and got introduced to a Detective Smith. He said that Carl and two more boys were in the mall trying to take money from another boy and that Carl had hit the boy. After taking Carl's statement, the Detective took us to a small room and had a conference with Carl. It humbled my heart to see this white man take the time to really talk with my son in the kind manner that he did. He appeared to be very sincere in not wanting to see Carl go down the road of trouble. Before departing Luke and I both expressed our gratitude to the detective.

As a result of that incident, Carl had to attend Juvenile Court. He was given six month probation with the requirement of washing police cars every Saturday. I had thought that incident would surely be a blessing in disguise and would have a significant change in Carl's behavior…no such luck. I was totally surprised by Carl's actions.

Carl, who had always been my quiet, sweet baby-boy; Carl, who year after year, would remain silent, and look on with disgust when his parents were demonstrating all that aggressiveness and disruptive behavior, had only been digesting it all, and was now letting it come forth. Therefore, I was on my desperate journey again, seeking Reverend Hunt's counseling, only now it was for Carl. I also increased Carl's church activities. But nothing seemed to help. His behavior at school was escalating, and I couldn't find a way to combat it.

Life became so intense that while at work, I regretted having to return home. A home is supposed to be your place of refuge, a place of enjoyment. But I considered mine barely endurable. And it never dawned on me that Jeff and Carl could have had those same feelings.

***

Saturday night at 9:30 p.m. Luke lost his house key and had to bang on the door. I ignored it.

He yelled repeatedly, "Open this motherfuckin' door!"

Jeff said, "Mama you might as well open the door. You see he is actin' a fool!"

Reluctantly, I finally opened the door, and came face to face with a red eyed, wild looking, deranged man.

Luke came toward me yelling, "What in the *hell* you mean, lockin' me out?"

Suddenly, Jeff jumped between us. "Daddy, don't you *hurt* my Mama!"

"I locked you out because I want you outta here!"

"If anybody goes, it'll be you!" shouted Luke, "You carry yo' motherfuckin' ass!"

"No!" I screamed, "You're gonna get out!"

"Bitch, put me out!"

"You get outta here right now!"

"Fuck you!" Luke shouted.

I screamed furiously, *"Fuck you, motherfucka!"*

At that moment, we were fiercely staring at each other like a rooster and a hen, waiting for the other to attack. And as reality would be, the "good girl" doesn't change the boy. The man had changed the woman ... I had become a hate-filled, frustrated wife.

Jeff, who was still between us, pleaded, "Mama, leave him alone. I'm so tired of y'all fussin' all the time!" His pleading voice and the look on his face, filled me with remorse.

An unemotional Carl just stared.

Guilt swept over me like a tsunami. I cried within, "Oh God! What am I doing to my children?" I wanted to hide myself, but the only solution that entered my mind was the police. I grabbed the telephone.

Quickly, Luke jerked the plug out from the wall socket.

With tears streaming from my eyes, stripped of my pride, I walked out of my house and went across the street to my neighbor's house. For the third time in our marriage, I called the police on Luke.

While at my neighbor's house, Jeff followed me and said, "Mama, you and Daddy need to do something. I'm so tired of all this fussin'!"

I felt the responsibility crowding on my conscience. But I gave Jeff all kinds of excuses as I cried out, "What do you mean, *we* need to do somethin'?" I continued, "Jeff, you know that I have begged and pleaded with your Daddy to leave and he will not. And I don't have any money to move into an apartment. It takes extra money to make a deposit and pay the first month's rent. I don't have anyone to go and live with! Now what do you want me to do?"

"I don't know Mama," said Jeff, "but y'all need to do something. I just can't continue to live at home with all this fussin' between you and daddy. I'm just *tired* of it!"

"Jeff, I'm tired of it too!" I said, "However, if you want to leave home, then you go." Jeff stared at me in frustration then walked out of my neighbor's house. In that gloomy moment, I felt that Jeff, too, held me responsible for all that had happened.

I remained in refuge at my neighbor's home until I saw the police arrive. Luke, seeing the policemen behind me, really became enraged as he started toward me saying, "Bitch, you call the police on me?"

An officer intervened and tried to calm Luke. But Jeff, Carl, and I watched as the officers had to use force with an out-of-control Luke.

Jeff, who moments earlier, had voiced his concern for me to his father, suddenly spoke out to the officers. He said sadly, "Why y'all got to do my daddy like that?"

They didn't respond as Luke was placed in the patrol wagon.

All alone in my room, I dissected my past. The image of Nannie's stretched eyes came to my remembrance saying, "Gurl! You love 'dat boy's *dirty drawers!*" I thought, *Nannie, if you were alive, now, I would tell you that I wished I'd never laid eyes on Luke nor his dirty drawers!*

I thought about Daddy's warning. "Girl, I know you think that you can change Luke, but I'm tellin' you from experience, that's not gonna happen." I said within, Daddy knew. Because no woman could change him! I thought, *If only I had listened! But Oh, no! My hard-headed ass just had to have Luke. Well, now I'm gettin' my belly filled of Luke!*

Things my Grandmama had said came back to me. I could almost hear her voice in my head: "Georgann, you can marry Luke, but he will never be the husband 'dat you want him to be. It jus' ain't in him. You can't 'git blood outta a turnip." Mama proclaimed, "Luke will *sour* on yo' stomach!"

I silently cried out, "Oh Mama! How right you were! Luke has not only soured on my stomach ... he has *clabbered*!"

Standing before the mirror, I shook my head and groaned. I didn't like what I saw. No longer was I the once considered "nice Christian girl." My mouth had become a filthy sewer. I thought about those years ago Bible reading sessions I had shared with Luke, trying to reform him from his bad habits. But it was I who had changed. Cusswords flies out of *my* mouth like bats outta hell! I cried out, "Oh Lord! What have I become? How did I let this happen? I'm destroying myself and my children. The time is now to take some action. Luke is in jail and I'm going to an attorney and start procedures on a legal separation. No more procrastinating."

Decision made, I drifted off into a peaceful sleep. At approximately 5 a.m., I thought I was dreaming, but the knock was repeated. I gave a distressful sigh as I staggered to the door and unlocked it. I returned to my bedroom in misery…all plans cancelled!

I felt then that I would never get Luke out of my life, and that he and I were destined to be *miserable* forever.

Defeated, I thought, o*h well, you might as well face it girl, you are stuck in this situation. You asked for it twenty-two years ago, so be content.*

I had appealed my sentence, but was denied my pardon before it even got to the Board, because of my bad behavior. So I had to remain in my cell to complete my time with Luke still handcuffed to me. However, the handcuffs had been placed around my neck, choking me. And I was gasping for breath ... slowly suffocating.

Later, Carl and I went to what I considered my refuge and solution ... church. My body was present but my mind was in complete chaos and utter confusion.

It was the hour for the sermon. Reverend Hunt, standing behind the pulpit said, "Open your Bibles to Philippians 4: 11-13." He read, "Not that I speak in respect of want, for I have learned, in whatsoever state I am, therewith to be content: I know both how to be abased, and I know how to abound: every where and in all things I am instructed both to be full and to be hunger, both to abound and to suffer need. I can do all things through Christ which strengthens me."

Through clench teeth, I mumbled under my breath, "I am *sicka* hearin' what Apostle Paul says!" I grunted, "Huh, I'm not Apostle Paul. I've tried to be contented, but I'm not! That's what's wrong with me now, tryin' to do what *Apostle Paul* says!"

My hand went to my chest and tears caught in the creases of the outer corner of my eyes as I prayed, pleading, "Lord, please help me! I'm so tired of this marriage. I'm trying to do what the Bible says, but Luke won't do what's right. When is he gonna change? Is he ever gonna change? – Oh, Lord! Please change Luke!" Suddenly I got confused and disgusted, and angrily said, "God, if this is what you want my life to be like, forever miserable, then help me to accept it!"

I should have stayed home that Sunday. The choir began singing one of my favorite songs, *"Trials dark on every hand. But there's a bright side somewhere."*

Disgusted, I said to myself, "I don't like that ol' *stupid* song! I don't foresee a bright side in my life! Only thing I can see is heartaches and pain!"

A burning knot formed in my throat, and my body wanted to succumb to the emotional outburst of hopelessness and frustration I felt. But, I tried to remain calm. I was suffocating, drowning in my emotions. When I came to myself, I was groaning and surrounded by two ushers. One was gently patting my back, and saying, "Georgann, Georgann, let it out!" The other one was fanning me, and said, "Chile, let the Holy Ghost have *its* way!"

※ ※ ※

On Monday, around 6:00 p.m., in the pastor's study, the room was filled with members getting their children registered for the computer literacy tutoring class. In the midst of all the commotion that surrounded me, I suddenly heard familiar, distinctive footsteps. I looked in the doorway and there was Luke. Reverend Hunt greeted Luke, and asked the others present to be excused.

"Mr. Dunbar, what can I do for you?" asked Reverend Hunt.

"Rev., my wife called the police on me for nuthin'," said Luke.

"Why would she do that?"

Luke began to give his version of what had taken place. As I sat there completely mortified I was so tired of all the turbulence in my life...I had tried to be the captain of my ship and navigate it to safety. But my passengers would not cooperate, and my ship was sinking, carrying me under.

I finally came out of my depressed state after hearing my pastor's voice saying, "When the situation gets so bad that it can become violent, there needs to be something done, before someone gets hurt."

"I know!" I said. "And I have begged Luke to leave, but he refuses to do so. There is no more love in this marriage, just misery!"

Luke abruptly jumped out of the chair and said, "I ain't leavin'! And ain't nobod' gonna *make* me leave!" Angrily, he burst out of the building.

The tears came streaming down my face as my mind wanted to yield itself into a dark and desolate place and I was fighting, trying to hang tough. I knew that if I allowed that to happen, I wasn't going to come back in my right mind. I'd be carried off to the funny farm!

Reverend Hunt said, "Sister Dunbar, you feel as if the situation is hopeless, don't you?"

My hand was covering my mouth, trying to muffle the grunts that were trying to escape from my throat. I nodded my head in silence as I sat there, feeling lost and alone. I was actually terrified to open my mouth because of the fear of losing my sanity.

He said, "There is always hope. It is up to you to make a decision. You pray and ask God for direction."

I thought, *Lord! I am praying about this situation, and I don't seem to be getting an answer! I just don't know what else I can do!*

Reverend Hunt prayed for me, but I was too distraught. Afterward, I took Carl, and carried my "basket-case" self home.

Tuesday, around 6 p.m., Luke not only appeared, but had an unexpected announcement.

He couldn't have had a more sincere look on his face when he said, "Georgann, I'm gonna give you what you want. I'll be leavin' here as soon as I find me a place to stay."

I gave a humble response. "I appreciate it." But my heart jumped with joy. Every muscle in my tense body relaxed. I could have done a holy dance! I said silently, "Oh, thank you Jesus!"

For the remainder of that week, I was experiencing euphoria. I couldn't have been any happier, other than receiving a million dollars.

I had assumed that come Friday, Luke would be leaving. Apparently, he had made other plans. A plan that he knew I wouldn't refuse.

Luke came directly home from work and gave me my million dollars...his paycheck!

In the meantime, Jeff retreated to Dallas again. Before his departure, I gave him another one of my lectures. On several occasions while in Dallas, he had gotten arrested for misdemeanors in addition to the seven months he had spent incarcerated before. I was always fearful of Jeff getting into some serious trouble in that city and my intuition led me to believe that eventually he would be sent to prison.

It wasn't long after Jeff's departure that Carl was to continue in Jeff's footsteps. Carl was suspended from school for fighting. Luke and I had to meet with a School Board official in the principal's office. It was like watching re-runs of an old movie, only the main character had changed. Now instead of Jeff, it was Carl. And, of course, I had summoned my pastor, Reverend Hunt, who has nothing better to do than be at the Dunbars' personal beck and call! Even so, the outcome was the same. Carl had to attend the school's alternative program. As a result, his grades improved tremendously and, thank God, he was promoted to the tenth grade!

Chapter 19
A Purposed Friend

January of 1987, was a cold and rainy month. Because of weather conditions, Luke was receiving $80 weekly in unemployment checks and I considered myself lucky if I received any of it. But I didn't complain. Because, after having what I considered so many storms and tornadoes in my life, finally some spring showers sprinkled on me. With God's blessings, I had managed and maintained my earnings well, and saved a little money weekly in the company's savings plan.

By March, the weather cleared. That week before Luke was to return to working, he gave me his solemn word, and even placed his hand on the Bible (but didn't fall to his knees) swearing that he was going to continue his weekly contributions to the household expenses. So, I bought another car through the Credit Union, and I let him have the Nova to drive. Lord, have mercy! That very first paycheck Luke received, he didn't come home. Luke had betrayed me again.

Sunday morning, Luke called. My temperature was blazing hot with anger. "Luke, you better bring my car home. If you don't, I'm going to the police!" I yelled into the telephone.

He replied, "You go to the police! But you ain't gettin' it!"

"No! It is not yo' car! It is mine, and you are not going to ride around freely in it. I paid for it, and the title is in my name!" I slammed the receiver down.

So, that beautiful, sun shining Sunday morning, I had no desire for church, and hearing about how God can solve your problems, and how Christians should have the fruit of the spirit. I stayed secluded in the house with the curtains drawn. I was tense, on edge, and listening for Luke with the car; Luke never showed.

Monday morning, I dragged myself out of bed. My chest and left arm were aching severely. My spirit was at its lowest. I drove to work anxious, fearful, disgusted, and carrying all that weight on my shoulders. I felt that I had no one's help, nor concern for me...I was drowning in self-pity.

Once I came upon my area, I was faced with another dilemma. There, sitting in the seat next to mine, was this little annoying five foot four inch woman. I thought, *Oh no! Not Reverend Joyce! I don't want to hear her talk about what the Bible says. Not this morning! I have too much on my mind and I definitely don't want to hear her... blah, blah, blah about God, because He has forgotten about me!*

Joyce was a force to be reckoned with. She was a poster child for God, and her motto was, "How *good*

God is!" Joyce's husband was a minister. I had thought cynically, *the Lord should have called HER instead of her husband! Now, of all mornings, why would she be sitting right beside me?*

With a mere "good morning" greeting to her, I began doing my work in silence. I tried to concentrate on doing my job but felt, at any given moment, I would actually jump up from my position and go running through the plant, screaming.

My mind was a mass of confusion, and I was not aware of the tears running down my cheeks. When out of a distance, I heard a voice calling me by my birth name, "Maple! Maple! What is the matter?"

In fear of becoming hysterical, I chose not to answer.

Her left hand reached over and gently touched my hand as she asked, "Maple, is there anything that I can do for you?"

I could barely whisper, "I don't want to bother you with my personal problems."

Speaking so kindly, Joyce said, "You will not be bothering me. Because, if there is anything I can do to help you, I would gladly do it," she continued. "We can't live in this world by ourselves. We are supposed to help one another!"

I looked in her face and discovered sincerity in her. And Lord, that's all it took! The tears really began flowing from my eyes.

As a result, I gave her a scenario of 22 years of my turbulent life to the present. She allowed me to unload all my burdens on her, uninterrupted.

When I finished, I looked into her astonished face. And for some reason, I felt the need to apologize.

"I'm sorry!" I said, "I didn't mean to bring my personal problems to work."

"Chile!" she gasped, *"you can't help to bring your problems to work. You're walking around in cement!"*

Those well put words and her facial expression suddenly became funny and we both began to laugh. I thought, *Well, Lord! There is still hope for me if I can still laugh in the midst of adversity.*

Luke came home that Friday evening with the car. Our relationship resumed as usual...shabby and meaningless, with me not seeing any way out of it.

At this point, I was always angry, tense... expecting trouble and like a time bomb, ready to explode at any moment.I had developed a nervous twitch in my left eye. My upper body was just one big tight rubber band.

***

That same month of March, Luke's shifty eyes showed fear when he showed me his swollen testis, and told me that he had lifted something too heavy on his job. At the age of forty-two, I was still as dumb and naïve as I was at thirty-two when Luke had told me he got crab louse from dirt and sweat!

Luke asked, "Will you go wit me to a private doctor?"

Being the "dumb-dumb that I was", I made Luke an appointment and accompanied him like the dutiful wife.

After our arrival, Luke wanted to speak with the doctor in private.

My curiosity was provoked.

Minutes later, Luke appeared. Eyeing him suspiciously, I asked, "Why did you have to speak with the doctor in private?"

Luke reluctantly said, "I told the doctor that I've been using drugs and was goin' to a free clinic where they take a urine specimen once a week to make sure I stay clean."

I gasped out in shock, "You been using what!?"

Luke said, "My problem ain't bad. I just smoke a little marijuana."

To this day I don't know why I was shocked. I had suspected that Luke smoked marijuana although he had never, to my knowledge, smoked it in my presence. I had accused him of it on several occasions…what I had called those ol' "funny cigarettes, or "that mess."

Perhaps, by Luke's admission and putting a name to it, for me, was a problem that I didn't want to deal with…and I had believed so many lies I didn't know what reality was. So when Luke said it wasn't a big deal, I believed him.

Luke had to have surgery and was admitted to the hospital for three days. Afterward, I brought him home for convalescence. Later that same day, he left and did not return. The next evening after getting home from work, I found Luke sound asleep and no car in sight.

I called out Luke's name. Luke didn't respond. For several minutes, I shook him, I pulled at his body, and I yelled in his ear.

Finally, he woke up and was incoherent, appearing to be in a daze.

"Luke," I asked, "where's the car?" I repeated twice.

Luke gave me a vague stare, and finally said, "I had a wreck in it last night and I had to leave it at this guy's house."

"Why did you have to leave it?"

"I ran a red light and hit this guy's car," said Luke. "We knew each other, and when the police came, instead of writing an accident report, he allowed us to settle it between the two of us. So I had to let the guy keep yo' car until I can pay for the damage done to his car."

"What about my car? Is it damaged badly?"

He quickly replied, "Oh no! Yo' car ain't hurt."

"How much is it going to cost for the damage done to his car?"

"It's gonna cost $210."

I sighed wearily, and said, "He will have to wait until next month when our income tax refund comes."

I suddenly became inquisitive and said to Luke, "Take me to my car." Luke highly protested, but, upon my insistence, he finally agreed.

I really became suspicious after seeing my car parked in the stranger's back yard along with some others with no visible signs of an accident. Nevertheless, that following month, the stranger was paid, and the Nova was returned. Life continued rolling on as usual, one thing after another. If one good thing happened, two bad things would happen right behind.

***

After six weeks recovery, Luke went back to work. Three weeks later he was fired. Within the same month of May, Jeff called from Dallas. He was in jail for a misdemeanor. I threw my hands in the air.

Had it not been for Joyce, who had now become my confidante and sister in the Lord, I don't believe I could have sustained. Joyce's faith was as strong as a steel beam that could hold up a house in an earthquake. My faith was as *shaky* as that earthquake! Her prayers and assurances that God wasn't going to put any more on me than I could bear was encouragement. Although there were times when I thought, *God might not put any more on me than I can bear, but the DEVIL sure in the HELL is!*

***

The second Saturday night in June, Luke left and returned Sunday morning without the car, again. His excuse was that the brakes had gone out, and he was going to get the brakes fixed as soon as he got the money. I felt he was lying, but I didn't say anything.

In July, I had two weeks off for vacation. I had promised Carl I would get him a lawn mower as a reward for doing well in the school's alternative program.

I went to my credit union and made a small loan. Later that same day, Luke and I went shopping, and found Carl a used self-propelled lawn mower in superb condition.

Carl's excitement filled over as he hugged me saying, "Oh Mama! Thank You! Now I can make me some money during the summer!"

Since I was on a roll, I asked Luke, "How much is it gonna cost to get the car?" Without any hesitation, he answered, "forty-two dollars."

I definitely knew then that the brakes had not gone out in the car. He had lied and pawned the car.

I didn't say anything other than, "Let's go get it!"

Within fifteen minutes after returning home with the car, Luke received a telephone call. His boss wanted him back at work.

I said to Luke, "Isn't God great? He has allowed three good things to happen in a day! I was granted the loan to buy Carl the lawn mower. Then we got the car back. Now your boss is allowing you to return to your job! Can't you see the blessings of the Lord?" I asked.

"Yes," Luke said, "I know what you mean and I thank God too!"

I was so jubilant because of the blessings God had allowed to happen that one day; it gave me the assurance that Luke couldn't help but change his ways after recognizing the blessings and goodness of God. And to beat it all, I suddenly got *fever on the brain*! After all that had happened, I even thought about trying to mend our broken marriage. I actually had the audacity to believe one day of blessings had changed Luke!

***

Tuesday morning, I made sure that Luke had everything a hard-working man needed; a full breakfast, prepared lunch, a carton of cigarettes, and twenty dollars in his pocket. I was thinking that if Luke's boss gave him another opportunity at his job, why can't I give him another chance at our marriage? For three days, I found solace in that thought.

Not only did my heart and my spirit feel at peace with Luke, but also by the church's two week Wednesday morning Prayer Meeting and Bible Study on God's Holy Spirit, which coincided with my two weeks vacation. The first Wednesday morning was a few regular members, and a mysterious visitor, he was a man who looked to be in his late thirties. He didn't say much, but when he did, he spoke with much authority and knowledge concerning the Bible and the Gifts of the Holy Spirit. He said God had given him the gift of "Laying on Hands." I didn't fully understand what he meant but accepted it to mean that he had the power through God to heal people. I was impressed with him and felt he did possess a special gift.

All that week, my spirits were so high that if I had had wings, I would have been stuck to the ceiling. Then came Friday, and I knew Luke would be late getting home because of cashing his check. So, I settled down in the living room in my same old chair.

The 5:30 p.m. news report came on television. I watched it in a relaxed mood. The 6:00 p.m. news came on and went off. I became somewhat concerned but was still a little optimistic. Around 8:00 p.m., I don't remember turning off the television, but I must have because Carl came in to find me just sitting there in the dark.

I remember him looking at me curiously and asking, "Mama, are you alright?"

"Yes," I mumbled with a heavy sigh, "I'm alright."

Carl was satisfied and went to his room. I sat in the dark, staring at the lighted clock on the wall as it went ... tick tock, tick tock, wishing I could stop the time in Luke's favor.

As the time grew later and later, I was still hopeful, and thought that Luke surely wouldn't betray me with his first back-to-work paycheck, after all that I had done for him! I pleaded, "Lord, please don't let this be happening to me again!"

I said aloud in anger, "Why do I keep allowing Luke to make a fool of me! I'm so stupid!" But I was still hoping...

By 9:00 p.m., I took a deep breath, with barely a whisper I spoke out, "Well Lord, Luke is not coming home... not tonight!"

For one week I had allowed myself to live in a world based on an illusion. When the realization slowly set in, I collapsed into a state of depression. I felt as if I had taken a big balloon and exhausted all my energy to blow it up and made a knot at the end of it. I get satisfaction from the task that I had accomplished, then all the air slowly leaks out. That's how I felt ... emotionally exhausted, deflated and suicidal. My mind went into a dark place and I had a dreadful, unspeakable thought. A strange voice spoke, "Why don't you just kill yourself? It would be so easy. Just turn on the gas stove and stick your head in the oven and die. You might as well. You can't get Luke to act right. He keeps betraying you. Your son Jeff is in jail. He won't act right. So, what are you living for? Your life is just meaningless ...nothing!"

While entertaining those thoughts, Carl came into my mind. I cried out, "Oh Lord! I can't do that! What would happen to Carl? He needs me. I can't depend on Luke to raise him. Luke's life is a mess itself! I owe Carl the benefit of having the right to be brought up with good moral values. Even though he is having his problems, there's still hope for him. If I had failed Jeff, I still have to do my best by Carl."

After sitting there in that same position until about 1:00 a.m., I finally came out of my deep black hole of despair, and when I tried to get out of the chair, I could not move. I placed both hands on the arm supports of the chair and tried to push myself up. It became impossible.

I panicked, and cried out, "Oh, God! I can't get up from this chair!" I knew my mind was playing tricks on me. Anyone should be able to get up out of a chair! I knew that I wasn't disabled. So what was the problem? Every time I attempted to get up, my arms became limp, and I just did not have the strength.

Seemingly, my favorite chair, with its big thick arm supports that had embraced and comforted me through grief, heartaches, and moments of anguish, now suddenly became my enemy, holding me in captivity...refusing to release me.

Frightened, again I cried out, "Oh, God! Please help me!" Then a small voice inside my head whispered, "You can do it, keep trying!" I made several attempts...nothing happened.

Finally, after the last cry to God for help, the voice said, "Now, go on. You can get up from this chair!"I felt energy coming back into my body. My mind was precariously close to insanity, had I not won the battle. It became apparently clear, for my survival I had to once again, build a defense mechanism for myself. And that was...hostile silence.

Sunday night, Luke came in apologizing, "Georgann, I'm so sorry!" He pleaded.

Sighing wearily, I said, "Luke, it's alright."

I was so sick and tired of him being apologetic and continuously doing the same thing. I tried to program my mind into believing that it didn't matter anymore, and that I was fine.

Monday morning, I went on strike. Luke had to fend for himself. But, at supper time he sat down to dinner as normal, but with no backlash from me.

Wednesday, I was in my last week of vacation and back to reality. I attended Bible Study and the mysterious visitor was back. Upon impulse, I made my acquaintance with him before leaving the church.

Chapter 20
The Spiritual Experiences

Thursday morning, July 9, 1987, at approximately eleven-thirty, I was alone in the house. After completing my chores, I settled down in the living room, in that same old chair and watched as the sun beamed in through the front screen door.

"It's such a beautiful morning," I thought, as I sat before the blank television. The silence around me put me into an even more depressed state where I was drowning in self-pity. With a heavy heart, I picked up my much-used, and faded twenty-three year old wedding gift from mama, and said to myself, "Mama, you were right when you thrust this Bible in my hands on my wedding night and said, Here, Chile, you gonna need this!" Mama's Bible's gift not only had been used as a substitute for my bridal bouquet, but now it had become my life jacket. So many times I felt that I was in a big sea, and the waves of the current were taking me under, but my life jacket was what saved me. However, at this moment, the Bible seemed to fail me as I turned page after page, trying to find some comforting words. I could only stare blankly at the pages.

Suddenly, I put the Bible down and went into my bedroom, with my heart and head pounding rapidly, seemingly about to explode.

I fell to my knees at the foot of my bed and began sobbing. I sobbed, sobbed, and sobbed. "Oh Lord! Please help me!"

I threw both hands in the air as I surrendered myself.

I pleaded again, in broken sobs, "Lord, I have done all I know how to do and have no one else to turn to but you. Please dear Lord, help me!"

My hands were still reaching up into the air and I was sobbing convulsively when instantly, the most incredible and awesome thing happened. A distinct voice spoke out, loud and clear, saying, "I'M WITH YOU, GEORGANN!"

Instantly, my heart began leaping with joy. I felt a "presence" in my midst.

I began clapping my hands in mystical exaltation, and saying, "Oh, thank you Jesus! Thank you, God! Oh, praise your name!"

Then a small inner voice asked, "What are you praising God for?"

I abruptly stopped my praises, clapping, and became uncertain. Suddenly I hear a musical chime … then still silence. Next, a warm breeze blew on me. It was like a warm breath of air. It covered my entire body from head to feet.

I looked up, then around to see where it was coming from. The window was closed and all I saw was the sunlight beaming through the curtains.

Then, I was certain that it was God's Holy Spirit that had spoken and breathed on me.

I started clapping and praising God again. However, that was not the end of that awesome event. In the midst of my praising God, something arose in the bottom of my stomach and began to make its way up to my throat.

I was astounded and began trembling with fright, as a small voice said, "If you open your mouth again, something is going to come out of it, that you don't understand!" I became even more frightened and refused to continue praising God.

Then my mouth seemed to take on a force of its own…wanting to open and I was fighting to keep it closed. But that sound refused to be silent. It finally forced itself out of my mouth and I was making a strange noise…a sound that I had never heard before.

My neck and head also began moving in a peculiar way and I could not control it. After seconds, it stopped. I was spellbound!

I remained on my knees, trying to rationalize what had happened. I didn't fully understand, but knew that it was a supernatural experience. I was awed, and amazed by God's sovereignty and omnipotence. A feeling of overwhelming reverence came upon me as I wept, joyfully. I could still feel *that* presence, which brought a serenity I had never felt before. I was humble, at peace and kept a song of praise in my heart for the remainder of that day.

Luke did not come home that Thursday or Friday. But, for the first time in years, I was at peace. I knew that God was in control and that He was with me.

***

Saturday morning, I quickly came down from my spiritual high, and was my old carnal-minded self when Luke called. "Georgann, do you know Reverend Hunt's telephone number?"

"No," I answered, "I sure don't."

"Would you give me an insurance form, so that I can go into the hospital?"

"No, I won't!" I said coldly. "If you need to go into the hospital, you go to LSU Medical Center, because you're not using my insurance!"

"Thank you," said a very polite Luke.

I said suspiciously, "What is Luke pulling now? I bet there isn't anything physically wrong with him. He just wants my sympathy! Well, I'm not going to feel sorry for him. Not this time! I don't care what he says the problem is. It will not bother me!"

Sunday morning, Carl and I went to church. Five o'clock that evening, an unfamiliar voice said, "I would like to speak to Mrs. Dunbar."

"This is Mrs. Dunbar,"

"I'm a doctor at the hospital where your husband came Saturday morning to admit himself."

"Admit himself," I repeated, "For what?"

"Your husband has a drug problem."

My heart began pounding rapidly, "What kind of drug problem?"

Reluctantly the doctor answered, "He's on cocaine."

"Cocaine!" I yelled.

"Yes, Mrs. Dunbar," the doctor said. "Luke has a cocaine addiction."

I got the most empty and sick feeling in the pit of my stomach. I didn't want to hear that word, "Cocaine."

The doctor said, "If Luke shows up, tell him that we are still waiting for him to return to the hospital."

The next day, while at work, I called the hospital. Luke had returned and admitted himself.

Driving to the hospital, my inner voice spoke loudly and clearly. *"Now, this is your way out of this terrible marriage."*

Luke's counselor greeted me. "Mrs. Dunbar, what you may hear from your husband might not be pleasant to you. He has informed me of how the situation stands with your marriage," she said with empathy. "It is your decision whether to stay or not."

Silently I followed her down the hall to a room called Detox. I didn't know its meaning nor had I ever heard the word before. With a sinking feeling, I realized a whole new world was about to unfold before me and I dreaded it. I couldn't bury my head in the sand any longer!

As we entered the room, Luke looked sheepish.

Trying to be cheerful, I asked, "How do you feel, Luke?"

He sighed heavily and looked down at the floor, "I'm on cocaine."

My pounding heart raced faster than normal. Just the thought of that dreadful word "cocaine", and what it represented, made my feet want to run as fast as they could from that room. But my heart would not let me.

The counselor left us alone.

Luke said, "I woke up Saturday morning on a parking lot and didn't remember how I got there. That's when I knew that I needed help."

There was silence. I suddenly remembered and my eyes narrowed. Since Luke was confessing, I asked, "So there never was any wreck in the Nova when I paid that man $210 to get it back?"

Luke's eyes remained fixed on that dull gray floor tile. "Naw Ann, the man was a drug dealer."

"A drug dealer!" I snapped, "Why did he have my car?"

"He took the car 'cause I owed him money for drugs."

My emotions went haywire. I felt contempt, disgust, and anger, knowing Luke and his drug supplier had swindled me out of that money.

While Luke was talking, my mind was traveling at a speed of one hundred miles an hour. I thought about the mountains that he had put before me, the curves he had thrown at me, the hills I have been afraid to go over, and the valleys that I have felt so lost in! I thought, *oh yes! But now the way is clear.*

Suddenly I remembered those marriage vows; "Through sickness and health, for better or worse."

Shit! I thought, *If only I didn't have a conscience!*

"Georgann," said Luke, "will you go tell my boss where I am and explain the situation to him?"

"Of course, I'll do that."

"Will you tell Reverend Hunt and ask him to pray for me?"

I agreed.

Luke's face really saddened as he said, "I don't know how I'm gonna explain this to Carl."

He really got my sympathy then. I said, "I'll explain it to Carl."

Luke finally raised-up his head. His eyes showed relief as he humbly said, "Thank you, Ann, I appreciate it."

The counselor returned, and informed me of the family group sessions on Tuesday, and suggested that Carl and I attend.

"Georgann," said Luke, "I'm so sorry! I never wanted you to know about this! I know that I 've put you through a lot and I swear I'm gonna get well and make it up to you!"

"You don't have to make it up to me. Just get yourself well."

Frankly, I didn't care to hear his promises. I had had a lifetime of them …unkept!

I left the hospital and made a visit to Luke's boss, and gave him the news about Luke. My next destination was home, which I dreaded the most.

"Carl," I said. "Come sit down in the living room. I have something to tell you about your father."

Carl, now fifteen years old, looked at me curiously and said, "What is it, Mama?"

I tried to explain to Carl about Luke's drug addiction as best I could, considering the fact that I didn't really understand it myself.

Carl got misty-eyed and looked sad, but never spoke. He agreed to attend the family group session, and that was that.

Jeff, who was still incarcerated in Dallas, called. I informed him about Luke's condition.

"Oh, yeah," was Jeff's only comment, which had me wondering, had Jeff known?

***

That Tuesday night of July 14, 1987, Carl and I attended our first group session, but my heart wasn't in it. I had become so bitter and heart-hardened. However, reality stared me in the face. As I sat listening to all the different addicts and their stories, I scrunched up my forehead ... *Sniffing glue, aerosol house spray, finger nail polish!* I thought, *Oh my God! How outlandish! I've never heard of such! People don't do things like that!* My mouth a gaped... shocked.

Luke's counselor had suggested that he stay in treatment for thirty days. However, on his fourteenth day, Luke decided that he was cured of his drug addiction and signed himself out of treatment against his counselor's advice. He returned home and to his job. That Friday, Luke attended one Alcoholics Anonymous meeting, and had not been back. Three weeks out of rehab, that Friday around seven o'clock p.m., Luke said, "Georgann, I'm going out. I'll be back later."

Like an old "mother hen" I said, "Okay Luke, but you don't need to be hanging around that same old crowd that you once hung with."

He said, "I ain't going 'round them! You think I'm crazy?"

"No," I said, "I just wanted to make sure that you don't forget."

Luke left.

At approximately one o'clock a.m., I was awakened abruptly by a noise under the carport where the storage house was connected. I started to investigate it but I thought to myself, "It is probably that old dog that has been trespassing in the neighborhood." I drifted back off to sleep, not giving it a second thought.

Saturday morning around six o'clock a.m., Luke came home after having been gone all night.

I arose early and prepared breakfast. Afterwards Carl said, "Mama, I'm gonna take the lawn mower and find me some yards to cut."

"Okay son, that's a good idea."

Carl went to get the lawn mower out of the storage house as I went about my housework. Suddenly there was a loud yell from Carl, "Mama! Mama! Come here!"

I ran out of the kitchen door to the storage house and found Carl standing with the door open. With tears in his eyes, Carl cried, "Mama, my lawn mower is gone!"

My heart sank.

Luke appeared, "What's the matter?" he asked.

"Someone took Carl's lawn mower!"

"Oh yeah?" said Luke.

"Yes!" I said angrily. "It probably happened when I heard this noise out here last night, but didn't get up to investigate. If I had followed my first mind, I would have caught that thief!"

Luke suddenly looked very sheepish and his eyes shifted and would not look directly into mine. An unpleasant thought crept into my mind. I cried inwardly, "Lord, take that suspicion from my mind! Surely Luke wouldn't take his own son's lawn mower!" Not only was the lawn mower gone, but the electric edger also.

I told Carl, who looked so disappointed, that I would buy him another mower and edger. And I kept my promise.

That was the weekend of Luke's reinstatement into the streets.

***

Saturday, three weeks after the stolen lawn mower and edger incident, we had a surprise visitor. One of

Luke's former street "homies" and his wife returned home from another state for a visit.

He and Luke were chatting away, reminiscing and revealing unknown secrets about the "good old days," when they drove to Dallas, Texas on weekends, transporting and transacting drugs and money.

I sat there in my living room, shocked. I had no idea that I had been living in the same house with a drug dealer! Within that hour, I was really getting an education on what I had "slept" through all those years. But, as I sat listening, my mind drifted back to those earlier years in the seventies. People knocking at the door at odd hours of night, that gallon bag of marijuana hidden behind the hot water tank, which Luke said was alfalfa. Then, there was the time that Luke stayed away from home an entire week, came home that Saturday morning, bubbling with excitement.

"Georgann," said Luke, "do you know where I've been?"

I gave him a cold stare and snapped, "No, I don't know where you've been, because I don't care!"

Luke rolled up the left sleeve of his shirt and said, "I've done what no other nigga that I *know* can say they've done!" he boasted, "I got off them drugs by myself!"

I was in my "don't-give-a-damn-state", and only glanced at his arm. And, being my dumb self, I tried to be smart-mouthed. I said, "All I see is a mark inside yo' elbow." I had said to myself, *He's just lying. He hasn't been shooting no needle in his arm!*

But, as I continued listening as the two old friends talked and talked, Luke's confessions caused my face to frown, and at that moment, I had a self-talk. "How could I have lived in the same house with Luke for twenty plus years, and not have known of his drug activities? I couldn't have been that dumb and naïve!" I shook my head, curved my lips downward, and said to myself, "Yeah girl, you knew something was going on. When doing Luke's laundry, you occasionally found in his pants pockets those tiniest clear button bags with the residue of white powdery substance. You couldn't have thought it was...*baking powder*! You just didn't want to face it. Truth be told, you have been living your life in denial!"Luke and his "homie" conversation changed to their present life. Luke's homie said, "Man, that street life almost killed me! I got off them drugs. Now all I do is go to church, to the movies, and restaurants with my wife."

Luke boasted, "Man, I know what you mean. I'm gettin' my life back together now! All I do is stay at home on weekends and have a few beers every now and then."

I cut my eyes at Luke.

Then neighborhood crimes became their topic of conversation, and suddenly Luke said, "Oh, by the way Georgann, I found out where our lawn mower and edger is!"

Surprised, I asked, "Where is it Luke?"

He said, "A guy told me about this man that manages a flea market that buys lawn mowers from anyone. I went by there to check and see if ours were there, and I found it there along with the edger."

I said excitedly, "Well, why didn't you get it?"

"I just can't get it," Luke said. "We will have to buy it from him! The man will hold both of them for me until I bring him $65.

Quickly, I said, "Let's go and report it to the police, so that we can get them back, free."

Luke interjected, "Now, wait a minute! You gonna mess things up! The man gave me his word that he would keep them until I brought him the money. If you go involvin' the police, he will get rid of 'em." Hesitating and thinking fast, Luke continued, "Anyway, we don't have the serial numbers on them."

"Getting the serial numbers wouldn't be a problem. I can go to the shop where they were purchased and get the numbers," I said.

"Oh, no!" said Luke. "Let me handle this! I will get them back as soon as possible!"

Suddenly it clicked...Luke was the thief!

In spite of this, I tried to continue being sociable and disguise my disgust. *I won't dwell on this one incident,* I thought *I will put this behind me and go forward. Having Luke's friend stop by is probably a blessing that will inspire Luke to change.* And, sure enough, when our visitor left, Luke was so enthusiastic. He said to me, "If he can change, I know I can!" He made an ardent vow that he was going to turn his life around.

Meanwhile, Jeff telephoned and said the charges against him had been dropped, and that he wanted to come back home. We drove to Dallas that next weekend and got him.

***

Luke's vow of making a change in his life became true. Only, it was the opposite. Luke worsened. I silently observed his pattern of behavior returning within three months. The Friday finally came when Luke seemingly could not contain himself. He didn't return home until that Sunday night and he looked guilty, hopeless and despondent. I also returned to my former state…hostile silence.

***

Thursday morning, October 8, 1987, approximately three months after Luke's unwise decision to free himself from the drug treatment program, he also volunteered unexpectedly and gave me my freedom...I took a deep sigh of relief. When he did depart, I still wasn't satisfied. Luke and I had been separated one week, when I *just happened* to spot him at a corner store that was known for its drug activities. Seeing Luke hanging around on that corner and knowing undisputedly that he was a drug addict brought about ambivalent feelings toward him. I felt sorry for him and angry with him for just giving up. Well as usual, I couldn't resist the opportunity to do something *really* dumb ...I approached Luke.

I said angrily, "Why are you hangin' around on this corner? Why don't you try and get your life together?"

"Why don't you quit downin' me and help me?" he accused.

Well, that's all it took. I drove off with Luke standing there looking helpless. Now, not only was I angry with Luke, but confusion and guilt were doing a number on me! Luke's pitiful look kept me in turmoil all night. By that next morning, I had made a definite decision to find someone to help Luke. I felt that Luke needed a strong Christian to take him under his or her wings and have prayers and Bible Study with him.

Then I remembered the mysterious visitor who had that gift of "Laying on Hands." I knew that he would be the perfect person that Luke needed. He would be able to perform that "miraculous miracle", and Luke would become healed from those drugs. I became desperate to find the stranger.

The next day at work, I inquired of the stranger from a lady who attended the same church. I had forgotten his name, but with my description of him, her eyes lit up. "Brother Henry," she said, "He is a spirit-filled Christian."

My heart leaped with joy as she promised to give him my message.

By the following week, I still hadn't contacted Brother Henry. That night I prayed, pleading to God to please send someone to help Luke--soon! The next morning, I thought about Mrs. Mattie, a member of my church. I heard she worked at a hospital and often gave spiritual counseling to her patients.After work I was desperately knocking on Mrs. Mattie's door. She agreed to counsel Luke there at her home for free. My plans were to initiate the counseling sessions for Luke. Afterward, he would be on his own.

Saturday evening, I picked Luke up and drove him to Mrs. Mattie's home for his first counseling session. Luke seemed immediately comfortable in her presence. Mrs. Mattie conducted her private counseling with Luke while I waited in another room. After the counseling, Luke appeared very jubilant and expressed how he looked forward to his next session. I took Luke back to his mother's home, with him still expressing his happiness of being helped. But, my mission was not complete. I was still eagerly waiting to hear from Brother Henry. The Wednesday night of that next week, my prayers were answered.

"Mrs. Dunbar, this is Brother Henry. I got your message and would like to meet with you and your husband as soon as possible."

Excitedly I said, "Luke and I are separated. He lives with his mother. However, I would be glad to give you his telephone number and address."

Brother Henry asked, "Mrs. Dunbar would it produce a problem for you if Mr. Dunbar could come to your home and I could meet with the both of you?"

My heart sank! I thought, *Oh Lord! I don't want Luke comin' back here!*

Nevertheless, I reluctantly said, "No, I don't see a problem with that." But I thought, *Why do I have to be included? Luke is the one that needs the help!*

We made the agreement to meet at my house that Sunday night, following Luke's Saturday night meeting with Mrs. Mattie. I called Luke to inform him of the arrangements. He was, again excited.

***

That last Sunday night in October 1987, Luke arrived at seven o'clock. Ten minutes later, my anticipated guest arrived with his wife and son. We got acquainted, and afterward, Brother Henry gave his testimony of how God had saved and changed his life. I was simply amazed. I got excited and thought, *Oh, yes! He's the one!* There was no doubt that God had sent him to us and was going to be the inspiration that Luke needed. Between him and Mrs. Snead, Luke was going to be healed of those drugs!

I was pleased with myself; everything was going as planned! I had it all under control. Luke was getting the help that he needed, Carl's behavior in school was stabilized, and I finally dismissed my paranoid notion that I was being punished by God. My faith in God was increasing, and I was finally at peace with myself.

But trouble loomed.

Chapter 21
The Revelation

In November, Jeff moved back home and was working the evening shift at a restaurant and felt he needed his own transportation. He solicited my help.

In my efforts to appease Jeff and because of my guilt for allowing him to quit school, I thought that having a car of his own would give him an incentive to keep a job, and follow through with his promise to enroll in Barber's School while getting his GED.

For those reasons, I went to the credit union and got a loan for Jeff's car. A 1984 red, five speed Subaru, priced far above what I had anticipated; $5500 with the weekly notes of $36, deducted from my pay, in addition to my own car payment of $46 weekly. I had no problem with it because Jeff looked me in the eyes and made a pleading, sincere, no doubt promise that I would be reimbursed weekly, and that he was going to enroll in barbering school, while also getting his GED. Out of guilt, I bought into it.

***

That Monday night in November, the weather had drastically changed, and it was very cold. Standing outside the door, was a pitiful-looking Luke. He said, "Georgann, I got into an argument wit' Madear, and I left there. Could I have some blankets to keep me warm while I sleep in the car?"

The warning signal flashed and a voice in my head screamed, *"No! No! No!"* But I ignored it and allowed my heart to overrule again, and said to Luke, "You don't have to sleep in the car. You can come back here and sleep on the couch until you find a place to stay."

Luke's eyes lit up, and a grin stretched across his face so much so, until I thought his cheeks was going to burst!

Oh, Lord, have mercy! What a foolish mistake I made!

That first Friday back, Luke knowing me well, came directly home from work, and gave me his paycheck. I didn't refuse it, didn't question his finding himself another sleeping quarters; I snatched the signed check out of Luke's hand and bolted out the door, and burned the rubbers on my tires driving to the bank!

Luke did well for several Friday's. But, that fourth Friday morning, Luke left for work and did not return. It was an awakening. Luke had not changed and was not benefiting from all that was being done to help him.

I discovered, however, that it was I who had become the beneficiary of those meetings. I took

Luke's actions in stride and I did not become devastated. I was learning slowly to put things in God's hands.

Sunday afternoon, Carl and I returned home from church, and found Brother Henry with Luke in a private conference in the living room for about an hour. Upon leaving, Brother Henry said, "Sister Dunbar, I think my brother is going to be alright."

I wanted to be optimistic like Brother Henry, but Luke's drug dependency became more visible and obvious than ever before.

Luke's counseling sessions with Mrs. Mattie had ceased, but Brother Henry, who was steadfast and zealous, continued in his weekly efforts to help Luke. The irony of it all was that Luke prayed verbally, with emotions, as the tears ran down his cheeks, pleading for God's help. It seemed as if the more Luke pleaded...the more the drugs began to take hold of his life. Our efforts to help him proved to be more harmful than helpful. Luke went on a crash drug binge, and there was no recovery.

I was so thankful that my life had spiritually evolved and focused on the powers that be. If not, Luke's drug addiction would have driven my barely sound mind… to insanity. However, I still had a problem with putting all things that I had no control over into God hands, especially concerning Jeff.

Earlier during that week, I had two disturbing things to happen concerning Jeff. The first was that I had dreamt I was sitting high up in the balcony at a church looking down in a casket at a young man's body, and I took it to be Jeff. The next disturbance, I had intercepted a telephone message for Jeff concerning his employment.

***

That Saturday evening of December, Jeff rushed in saying, "Mama, I'm going to drive to Natchitoches, Louisiana with some friends to see the Christmas lights. I'll be back tomorrow."

Firmly I said, "You've lost another job, again, so that car stays put!"

"I already have another job. I'll start to work Monday," said Jeff. "I knew how you would react, so I didn't tell you."

I wasn't convinced he was being truthful, so I preached Jeff a sermon on his irresponsible ways and his unkept promise of returning to school. I demanded his car not be driven unless he was seeking employment.

Jeff said angrily, "Well I'm going to pack my clothes and leave! I can't stay here with you anymore because all *you* want to do is run my life!" He went into his room and minutes later he came out with his packed suitcase and was searching for his keys.

I said to Jeff, "You can leave but the car stays here." I had the keys in my hand.

Jeff exploded. "You can't take my car! That's my car and you can't take it from me!"

Jeff stood in a hostile position and looked ready to attack me at any moment. He yelled, "I am tired of you tryin' to run my life! You want to treat me like a little boy. I am no boy! I am a man. And I want to be treated like one!"

I blinked away a shocked look.

Luke suddenly jumped between us, and said angrily, "Don't talk to yo' Mama that way."

Jeff ignored him.

The confrontation between the two of us got even more vehement.

"Boy," said Luke, "I told you to stop talkin' to yo' Mama in that way! And I mean for you to stop it, right now!"

Then Luke calmed down and said with emphasis, "Jeff, that ain't yo' car. The payments are being taken out of *her* check. The car is in *her* name. Son it is *her* car and *she* can do with it whatever she *wants* to!"

What Luke said, and how Luke said it, gave me quite a jolt. I stared at them both, in total bewilderment. I thought, *My Lord! What is going on here in this house? Jeff and Luke both seemed to have contempt for me, with all my efforts to help them both.*

Jeff continued in a rage, and Luke could not make him settle down.

Hesitating and with reluctance, Luke said, "Jeff, if you don't calm down, we'll have to call the police!"

Jeff looked betrayed and said, "Daddy, I love you and Mama. You don't have to call the police on me, because I am leavin' here!"

Suddenly, my anger and bewilderment were over-shadowed by love for my son. I said, "Jeff, you don't have to leave."

"Yes Mama! I've got to leave here!"

Jeff started for the door with his suitcase, but I grabbed his arms. "Son, please don't go! We will work something out!"

With tears in his eyes, Jeff said, "Mama, you have got to let me grow up! You can't keep treatin' me like a child! I will be twenty-one years old in January!"

My heart was heavy with despair as I released him. I pleaded again, "Jeff, please go back in your room and think about what you're doing!"

He hesitated for a second then returned to his room with his suitcase.

Luke said, "I don't know what done got into that boy! He was really actin' crazy! If I hadn't been here, he might've tried to hurt you!"

The thought of Jeff trying to take those keys from me was inconceivable. My having grown up in the 50's and 60's and being taught that disrespecting your parents would shorten your days, I really became afraid for Jeff because of his disrespectful behavior toward me. I followed him into his room for an apology from him and to reconcile our differences.

As I sat beside him on his bed, I said, "Jeff, we need to talk."

Jeff nodded his head in frustration.

"What is the problem that we can't get along?" I asked.

Jeff looked at me with tears in his eyes and said, "Mama, I don't know. We just can't get along!"

Reluctantly, I told him about my dream.

He said, "Mama, if something is going to happen, it's going to happen!" At that point we were both weeping. I gathered him in my arms, clinging to him, and cried, "Jeff, I love you. I don't want anything to happen to you. But your act of disrespect toward me is very dangerous for you! Also, I will not have you talk to me that way again!"

Jeff said, "Mama I'm sorry. I didn't mean to say those things to you, but you just don't understand! You have got to allow me to grow up!"

I agreed, but I refused to give in to his request to leaving town.

Minutes later, Jeff called out from his room, "Mama, pick up the telephone."

I picked up the kitchen phone and lo and behold, Jeff had called for the preacher man! Reverend Hunt asked my permission to come immediately and talk with me. Within twenty minutes, he was knocking on my door.

Fearfully, I told Reverend Hunt about my dream.

He said, "Sister Dunbar, if something is going to happen to Jeff, you cannot prevent it from happening. Whatever destiny has in his path, it is going to take place, and there isn't anything that you can do about it. There are some things one has no control over." He continued, "Jeff is a young man now. Sometimes, mothers don't allow their children to grow up. When they are his age you shouldn't give them something and take it back, like we do little children. There comes a time when mothers have to let go of the apron string." So, with my prayers, Jeff went off to Natchitoches.

I was really trying to make God the center of my joy, as opposed to feeling downtrodden. I grew stronger with each crisis and they were coming, one after the other, often simultaneously. I was still in some ways timid, fearful and always expecting trouble within my household. Simply because there *always* was *trouble* in my household!

Luke, who was temporarily idle from work because of the weather conditions, hocked the car again to another guy. This time, I had no intentions of getting it out. It remained idle where it was parked, which was probably a blessing, because it didn't have any insurance coverage.

Luke had no means to support his habit, so he did whatever it took. For Carl's sixteenth birthday, I had bought him a Boom Box cassette player. One day when I came home from work, Carl met me at the door crying, "Mama, somebody took my Boom Box!"

Innocently, I said, "Jeff probably borrowed it and will bring it back soon."

But it wasn't Jeff, it was Luke, and he gave me one of his convincing stories. He had pawned the radio for money to pay for transportation to see about a job that paid $9 an hour.

Luke said, "Georgann, the Supervisor remembered me from years ago and knows that I am a good worker. He was even going to put me over the other workers. I had to go and take a physical. I had passed it, but afterwards he told me that I would have to fill out a work sheet, but I couldn't accept the job because I can't read!" Luke's eyes got misty, "I had that job in my hands, but knew I wouldn't be able to fill out those papers. I could have cried," he said convincingly.

Of course, Luke really had my sympathy. He promised to get Carl's radio back. That next week Luke was back working, and for once he kept his promise. Two weeks had gone by since Jeff visited Natchitoches, when he announced again, that he and some friends were driving to Dallas for the weekend. This was against my better judgment, mainly because the car needed maintenance work. However, Jeff, who was always a headstrong person, left town that Friday evening after getting off work. Saturday evening, I received a telephone call from him saying the clutch had gone out on the car, and the repair cost would be $250 at the most. He had to find a job. But he had left trouble in Shreveport.

***

Jeff had been in Dallas a week. That Sunday night, I received a phone call from a long-time acquaintance named Dorothy. She said, "Georgann, I hate to call with this problem, and I tried to wait to see if the matter would be taken care of without involving you!"

I said, "What is it, Dorothy?"

Reluctantly, she said, "My son let Jeff have my gun without my permission, and I must get it back. It is registered in my name and is a very expensive gun. I'm trying not to report it to the police, but if I don't get it back, I will have to go to them!"

Luke, who showed unusual interest in the conversation said, "Let me talk to Dorothy."

"Dorothy," said Luke, "the gun is in the pawn shop. Don't worry about it because I will take care of it and get it out this weekend."

I was already surprised by Dorothy's information, but became dumbfounded by Luke's. I spoke with Dorothy again, and apologized for Jeff's action, and I also assured her that she would get her gun back. I gave her my word in confidence.

Afterwards, Luke informed me that Jeff had secretly called him and told him to go and check on a gun that he had pawned, but Jeff supposedly had not revealed whose gun it was.

Luke said that Jeff could go back to jail if caught with a gun in his possession because he was a convicted felon.

Wearily, I asked, "How much does it cost to get the gun out of pawn?"

"Eighty dollars," Luke answered. "But don't worry. I will get it out this weekend!" promised Luke.

Frustrated, I thought, *what kind of person had I reared? Jeff had no regard for other people's property! Everything I have tried to teach him has just been in vain! I have just failed in raising Jeff!*

During that week Jeff called from Dallas. His excuse for taking Dorothy's gun was, "Mama, I needed the money for my trip here. I was going to get it back the next weekend!" Jeff had no remorse for his action.

Chapter 22
Undependence, from Codependency

That Thursday night, I reminded Luke of his promise to get Dorothy's gun out of the pawn shop. He reassured me that it would be taken care of. Friday morning Luke went to work, and did not return home.

In spite of all the effort Brother Henry was putting into trying to help Luke, his life was going downward. He didn't even bother to make excuses anymore. He just had free shelter. I realized we were losing our battle, but the war wasn't over yet. I wasn't ready to throw in the towel. Not yet!

Sunday morning Luke came home. His addiction was noticeably affecting his appearance. The loss of weight, and that red glassy look in his eyes. Nevertheless, I was glad to see Luke, for reassurance that he had gotten Dorothy's gun and taken it to her. I was so relieved, and the remainder of that week went on as usual, until that Sunday night.

"Georgann," said Dorothy, "I hate to disturb you again but I have not heard from Luke since I called the first time."

"What?" I yelled.

"Yes!" said Dorothy. "It's been two weeks, and I was trying to wait, because I know how a situation can be when money is involved, and I realize it takes time."

Bewildered, I said, "Dorothy, please forgive us! When Luke comes home, I will definitely find out what happened and give you a call!"

Dorothy, being a widow, then consoled me. "Georgann," she said, "you must remember, I've been married. I know you, and I know that you believe in doing what's right!"

"Thank you, Dorothy." I hung up the phone in dismay.

***

Monday morning, I went to work intensely distressed. I tried to keep my secret within, because I was so embarrassed about what Jeff had done. I didn't want to share that with anyone, not even my very close friend, Joyce.

However, I was consumed with anxiety and was about to explode. I had to let it out.

Afterward, Joyce, who always called me by my birth name, said, "Maple, you are doing all that you can for your family. You are not responsible for the things they do."

"But I have got to take care of this matter. If not, Jeff could go back to jail! I can't depend on Luke, so it is left up to me."

"You do whatever you feel you must do. But you have got to stop worrying about those *grown* people and take care of yourself!" said Joyce.

Monday evening Luke returned home.

"Luke,' I said, "you told me that the gun was taken care of."

"I did!" he responded. "I just didn't take it to Dorothy."

"Where is it?"

"I didn't have the money to get it out myself, so I got this white guy to get it out for me and I will get it from him this weekend," he explained. "Don't worry, it is outta' Jeff's name, and I will get it to Dorothy this weekend."

I telephoned Dorothy. Luke assured her that the gun was in responsible hands, and that it would definitely be in her possession by the weekend.

However, on Wednesday of that same week, a desperate Luke pawned Carl's Boom Box, again. I realized then that there never was a job offered Luke that required him to fill out any work sheet.

Carl's Boom Box was never returned. Christmas was that next week, and I purchased him another one.

In the meantime, Jeff phoned from Dallas requesting $50 so that he would be able to buy a pair of insulated work boots that were needed for his alleged second job. Of course, it was granted.

Needless to say, my stress level had intensified until it was virtually impossible to carry on a conversation with anyone without twitching my eye. I was at the point where I didn't know how long my mental condition would hold up. It was an effort every morning for me to get out of bed. If it had not been for Joyce, I don't believe I could have maintained!

She said, "Maple, pray, and turn things over to the Lord."

"I am praying, Joyce!" I cried.

"Yes! You are!" said Joyce. "But you are not completely giving your problems to God. You keep trying to solve them yourself. God doesn't need your help! When you give them to Him, let it go!"

***

January, 1988: I thought, *Lord! So much has happened this past year. Please let this year be better.* However, it started the same as the previous year ended. Luke was still blowing his entire paycheck. Jeff, who would become twenty-one years old on the 25th of that month, was still in Dallas. And Dorothy was still being patient.

***

By February, with money in my old black purse, I held it tightly under my arm. I took a deep breath as I stepped into that used car business office and faced a smiling man, who was ready to accommodate me with a car.

"What can I do for you today?" he asked.

"I'm Maple Dunbar, Luke's wife."

The man's smile faded. "Well, what is it you want?" said the man.

"Luke said you're holding a gun for him, and I came to get it."

The man looked puzzled. "Yes, I got the gun out of pawn for Luke, after he explained to me about his son's situation, plus I gave him $40 for the gun."

I saw his lips moving, but I didn't want to believe what I was hearing.

I tried to keep a straight face, "I came to pay you for the gun."

"I don't have the gun." He said, "I sold it!"

I felt like all the air had been sucked out of me. My shoulders drooped, and my head hung down, completely devastated. I thought, *Oh, Lord! I can't believe this! What am I going to do now? Luke had been lying all along!* I cried out, "How am I going to tell Dorothy?" The emptiest feeling came upon me and I just wanted to run away and hide. I painfully questioned myself, what kind of people am I living in this house with? First, my son got someone's property and pawned it, then his father pulls a fraud…Lord, have mercy! I thought, *there's no way I can fix this! I tried to get it taken care of, but it has gone beyond my reach. Dorothy has no other alternative under these circumstances, there's no choice but to report this to the proper authority. Even if it means Jeff's incarceration...she has no choice!*

I finally arrived at Dorothy's house. My chest was so tight and heavy with despair. I could barely put one foot in front of the other. I informed her of the situation; "Dorothy, do whatever you must," I concluded. "I understand yo' position and I would never hold any animosity against you. I realize you must do whatever is necessary for your protection."

Dorothy smiled, and to my amazement, she said, "Georgann, don't worry about it. I have prayed and given it to God. I know you have tried to do what you could, and I appreciate it. Remember, I have children too."

I stood there, as the tears formed in my eyes. I realized Dorothy was putting herself in jeopardy. Her Christianity and compassion were so obvious and I was humbly grateful to her as she made it known that she was doing that act of kindness because of me. I will forever appreciate her and her unselfishness. After expressing those sentiments to her, I departed from her home.

I drove to my house in deep despair. I felt responsible for Jeff's actions...he is my son, a product of myself. It was a reflection on me, as to his failure or success. I thought, *Lord, I tried to teach him to do what is right, but I have failed.*

I was overcome with nausea by Luke's lies and deceptions. I cried out, "Oh no! This is just too much! Luke has got to go! I can not take anymore of him! I am throwing in the towel!" I had gotten slammed into the wall of reality and came out of my eyes-wide-open coma; about the women, the lies, the betrayals, and the drugs, from my twenty-three years of being married to Luke. I couldn't sacrifice, deny, or overlook the truth any longer. In St. John 8:32, it reads, "And ye shall know the truth, and the truth shall make you free." I finally realized that I was never the best wife a man could have. But I was only the biggest fool Luke had! I could hear my grandmama's words. "Georgann, it ain't no sense in you being *'dat* bigga fool!"

***

Saturday evening, at 6 p.m., the faithful Brother Henry showed up. Luke had not been home since Thursday morning and I regretfully informed Brother Henry of my decision and my feeling that our endeavor with Luke had been fruitless.

Brother Henry said to me that all had not been in vain. He said, "Sister Dunbar, the seed has been planted. We have given Brother Dunbar God's word and prayers. Now it is up to him to accept it or to reject it. We have done what the Lord required of us."

I said, "I'm sorry that things turned out this way. I realized that you did all that you could have done to help Luke."

Suddenly Brother Henry smiled, as if he knew a secret and said, "Sister Dunbar, God knew from the beginning what was going to happen. It wasn't by chance that we met. God knew that you needed more faith and strength in Him than you had before we met." He continued, "My Sister, God heard your prayers about your husband a long time ago, but it wasn't time for Him to answer you then. There is a time for all things. Now is your time to step out on faith and get rid of that fear, which has held you in bondage and be bold for the Lord! God can use you in a mighty way, but Satan wants to suppress your witnessing for God. It is not your husband Satan is after, but you! Everything that Satan has thrown against you, your faith in God still stood. Even though it got shaky at times you still held on and tried to live for God. It is Satan's job to destroy that in whatever way he can, through your husband, your children, or whomever!"

In a receptive spirit, I could so vividly see what my brother in Christ had revealed. I quickly reflected over the events in my life. As a result, I fully recognized that it wasn't anything but the "Grace of God" that had sustained me.

That next Friday, Luke came through the door with his paycheck in his hand. It wasn't accepted. No amount of money Luke could ever give me would compensate for all the stress and mental anguish that had consumed my well-being and our marriage. Candidly, I wanted to say, "Nigga, take that *check* and cram it up yo' *goddamned ass*!" But, I remembered Ephesians 4:26-32, "Be angry, and do not sin," do not let the sun go down on your wrath." And "Let no corrupt word proceed out of our mouth," etc. Besides, all I wanted was PEACE!!!

***

Jeff, who had been in Dallas about six weeks, and was supposedly working two jobs, had called the week before, again requesting $150 to pay for repairs of his car, not considering the fact that his car payments were still being deducted from my check weekly. Nevertheless, I wired him the money along with an extra $40. He finally returned home and had to seek employment again.

Making a definite decision to end my marriage, I actually had no money to make the move, but I knew I had to do something. The only thing I had left was prayer, and I made it simple and sincere, as I bowed on my knees in submission.

"Well, Lord, it is left up to you, now! Only you know whether or not Luke is going to change. If he is not going to change in this marriage, get him out of my life!" And, for the first time, I really meant it. Afterward, I felt so much serenity. I knew that this matter was in God's hands. God had given me my wings through Brother Henry and Joyce, and now it was time for me to soar!

At four o'clock a.m., the alarm clock buzzed. I opened my Bible to St. Mark 11:22-26, and those verses took on a new meaning for me. I put my faith in action ... reading, praying, and anointing my door facings and rebuking Satan to get out of my house! Three mornings, I glanced down at Luke lying asleep on the couch and thought, *Why not?* The oil on my finger lightly touched the skin on his forehead, I whispered, "Satan, I rebuke you in the name of Jesus. Get out of this house!" After the completion of seven mornings, I stopped my oil ritual, but continued my prayers and Bible readings.

Tuesday, February 23, 1988: that night my inner spirit spoke to me. It was time to have a conference with Luke.

No anger, no resentment, not anymore...my heart felt at peace.

Unaccustomed to hearing the humbleness in my voice, Luke looked at me strangely when I asked, "Luke, would it be alright if I talk with you?"

Suspicious, Luke's eyes narrowed, "Yeah, it's alright."

I spoke in a matter-of-fact tone, "Luke, I've done all I know how to help you. I tried getting you help. We have prayed with you and for you. It looks as if everything we've done only made you become worse off than before."

Nodding his head, Luke looked pitiful.

I continued. "I know you have a drug addiction, but I can no longer accept living under these circumstances. I've given this marriage all I can give; I have nothing left. I'm not going to deal with your drug problem any longer and make my life miserable." In conclusion, I said boldly, "Luke, you are going to leave here!"

Luke became enraged.

"You leave!" Luke shouted, "Since you ain't satisfied. You carry yo' motherfuckin' ass! Cause ain't no motherfucka gonna put me outta here!"

With more boldness and certainty than I ever dared before, I remained calm. "Luke, I have put you into God hands," I said, "because I cannot carry this burden any longer and I don't believe that God wants me to continue living in this situation."

Luke's whole countenance changed. He said in a frightened voice, "I don't need you prayin' against me, now!"

"I am not prayin' against you. I don't want any harm to come to you. I only want you out of my life."

A quieter Luke repeated angrily, "I told you, ain't nobody gonna put me out of *this* motherfucka!"

With confidence and much authority, I said, "Oh yes! You're going to leave here! However, the choice is yours as to what way! You can leave by walking out or being carried out! You *are* going...one way or the other!"

Luke was totally dumbfounded.

I went into *my* bedroom, said *my* prayers, with *my* peaceful mind, and slipped off into a dream world!

When I returned home from work the next evening, Luke wasn't there.

Two days later, that Thursday, the 25th of February, after getting home from work, my body was relaxed and my spirit was at peace. That's when the telephone rang.

"Hello," I said.

"You don't have to pray against me now, 'cause I am outta yo' life!" said Luke.

Thinking it to be just a hoax, I said with a nonchalant attitude, "That's good, Luke."

But, Luke said in a frightened and urgent voice, "You can stop prayin' against me now. I mean it! I'm outta yo' life for *good*!" the telephone clicked.

I said to myself, "Luke is lying to me!"

I had *faith* that God was going to get Luke out of my life, but I had not expected it to be *that* soon. My pulse raced as I began to investigate.

I opened Luke's closet ... empty! I pulled out his dresser drawer ... empty! My mouth opened and froze in shock. I said aloud, "Please, Lord, let this be real!" I looked around the house, even in the storage house to make sure that Luke had not hidden his clothes. No clothes in sight! My hands went up in the air, clapping! My feet danced around in circles! "Oh, Lord! Thank You! Thank You! Thank you, Jesus!"

That night, as I fell to my knees in prayer, I could not thank God enough as the tears kept rolling down my cheeks. Like a beaming light, gratitude exuded from every part of my being. My "walking around in cement" which Joyce had so poignantly expressed, was a thing of the past. Now, I felt free!

The next morning, I hurriedly dressed for work to share my good news with Joyce. She hugged me and said, "Don't stop praying about things and reading your scriptures, because Satan is not through with this yet!"

I thought, *Why is Joyce saying that? Everything is going to be great now, just great.*

Chapter 23
Setting Myself Free

Luke and I had been separated over a month, and my mind and body were in an unfamiliar zone... I wasn't tense and filled with anxiety, and the twitching in my eye had disappeared as suddenly as it had appeared. It was really incredible how relaxed I had become. It was a blessing, and I thanked God daily.

I had planned to save my money for an attorney to get my separation. Then Jeff, who worked the evening shift, informed me that, while I was at work Luke had been making return visits...washing his laundry, eating food, watching television, and taking a bath. And was having Jeff to bring him there!

Luke's shenanigans were not going to be tolerated. That next Wednesday, I left work at eleven o'clock a.m. and walked into my house to find an unwelcome guest. I was pissed, but I kept my cool.

I asked, "Luke, why do you come here to wash yo' clothes? We are separated, and you shouldn't be coming back here!"

Luke's eyes narrowed. His pointed forefinger was inches from my face. "I can come back here whenever I want to!" said Luke, "and no motherfucka betta' not try to stop me, 'cause I will blow they *motherfunkin'* head off!"

Without responding, I walked out the door, got into my car, and drove to the police station, and applied for a restraining order on Luke.

Saturday morning, around noon, Jeff answered the telephone.

"Mama," said Jeff, "that was Daddy. He wants me to come get him and bring him here so that he can wash his clothes."

"Oh no, you are not!" I said, and I returned Luke's call.

I spoke harshly, "Luke, you know that you can't bring yo' clothes here, nor come here any more!"

"I will bring my clothes 'round there anytime I get ready!" snapped Luke.

"You are under a Peace Bond!"

"Fuck a peace bond!" he yelled. "I'm comin' 'round there now!" and slammed down the telephone receiver.

I became confused and out of sync.

Jeff was alarmed. "Mama, you had better call the police, because you know how crazy Daddy can get!"

I said, "I'm not calling the police because he is not coming around here. Luke is just blowin' wind!"

"Mama, I am tellin' you to call the police now! You know Daddy is on that stuff and there is no tellin' what he is going to do!" he warned. "And I don't want to be here when he comes cause' I'm tired of y'all arguin'!"

Calmly, I spoke, "Jeff, take Carl and leave, and I will call the police."

Jeff got Carl and drove off.

"Ma'am," said the dispatcher, "we can't do anything until he gets there. Then you call us back!"

I hung up the telephone, horrified. *Lord! Luke is going to have to kill me for them to come!* My body weakened, and my legs seemed as if they were going to crumble. I spoke aloud, "Oh, Lord! This is no time for me to get weak!" My heart was racing as I hurriedly locked the screen and wooden doors.

Suddenly, a calm inner voice spoke. "Why are you so afraid? Luke is just bluffing. If he comes here, he is not going to hurt you." Energy returned to my weak body as I went about doing my chores, calmly.

Ten minutes later, I heard a loud banging noise at the kitchen door and a voice yelling, "Open this *goddamn* door!"

I opened the wooden door, but the screen door remained hooked as I came face to face with a deranged man full of rage and violence…and I tried to reason with him! Help me, Jesus! It was useless. I threatened to call the police.

Luke yelled, "Call the motherfuckas, 'cause it's fixin' to be some trouble now!"

He snatched, and broke the hook on the screen door, and entered the house.

I dialed the number.

"Call 'em!" said Luke, "Call the motherfuckas!" As he went into the living room and quietly took a seat. Luke, the roaring lion, suddenly became a calmed lamb. He said, "You called the police. Now I'm gonna sit here and wait on 'em."

Minutes later, I invited the policeman inside with Luke still sitting in that same position.

The officer took my restraining papers, which showed that Luke and I were to appear in court the following Wednesday.

The officer was very courteous, and said in a mild tone, "Mr. Dunbar, you are not supposed to be here. So, would you please leave?"

Luke suddenly jumped up from the chair, shouting, "Take me to jail, motherfucka! That's what you come here for! Now, take me!"

"Man, I don't want to take you to jail," said the young black officer, "I just want to talk you into leaving here, without any trouble!" It was somewhat a plea, which only seemed to infuriate Luke even more.

"Motherfucka! Take me to jail!" Luke demanded. "That's what you wanna do! Take me!" said an enraged Luke.

The officer shook his head. Reluctantly, he said, "Okay, Mr. Dunbar! If that is what you want, then I will do it."

The officer and I were astounded by Luke, voluntarily placing his hands behind his back. The handcuffs were clamped on Luke's hands, and he was escorted to the patrol car. The officer returned and apologized. "Mrs. Dunbar, I don't know what is the matter with your husband but he seems to be about to explode!" He continued, "I didn't want to arrest him however, he insisted. And he wasn't going to leave so I had no choice."

***

Sunday morning as I sat in church, I prayed. Asking, begging, and pleading to the Lord to please get Luke out of my life. I just wanted to get out of this troublesome, miserable marriage and to have some peace in my life.

Monday evening, I searched the yellow pages, and found a reasonable lawyer. Tuesday evening, I applied for a loan with my reliable credit union and was told to call back Thursday. That same Tuesday night, I did my routine prayer and Bible reading, and I drifted off to sleep. My dream placed me in this small town called Greenwood, Louisiana. I was riding a bicycle, trying to get home, and as those similar dreams would be, I always came upon a fork in the road. This fork was three-pronged, and as usual, I became uncertain which road I should enter. However, at the end of the main road I was traveling on there were two white buildings on the right. One was a church building with a large group of ladies in choir robes, standing outside on the porch singing and clapping their hands, giving praises to God. The other building was an ordinary house where two ladies were outside, preparing food…getting ready for a feast! Both ladies were stout and big-busted. One was dark complexioned and the other was of lighter complexion. I thought *these two ladies look so familiar. I've seen them before, but where?* I approached them. "Miz, could you tell me which road I need to take to get me home?"

The first lady said, "You can take the left and it will get you home."

I looked out into that road and it had an immense amount of traffic. I said to her, "No I don't believe that I want to get on that road!"

The other one said, "Well, you can take the middle road. It will take you home."

I surveyed that road. It had no traffic, but was narrow, with lots of trees on the side, and the branches were overlapping the road. I gave the second lady the same response.

Then, I looked at the road on the right. There wasn't any traffic on it. It was a straight road, and finally, *finally* a road without a hill. I said to both of them, "I know what road I will take! I will take the right road. It will get me home!" Both ladies smiled and nodded their heads. I was confident as I excitedly hopped back onto my bicycle and started pedaling down that road, never looking back. I wasn't afraid anymore. And I had made the decision for myself!

***

Wednesday morning I awoke, never giving the dream any thought. I was preoccupied with thoughts of my 9:30 a.m. court appearance. This was required because of the Peace Bond that I had put on Luke, who was still in jail from Saturday's disturbance.

Before leaving the house, I got on my knees again, praying to God to please put an end to this turbulent marriage, and let me get on with my life. I drove to court full of confidence. However, once in the courtroom my confidence was shattered and I became shaky because of a similar case that preceded mine. The judge told the lady that her husband had just as much right to be in their home as she had because she had not filed for legal separation.

I became horrified. "Oh God!" I whispered, "He is going to tell me the same thing!" My mind began to scatter in all directions. But, within minutes, I remembered my prayer and my confidence restored...God was still in control!

Our case was next. Luke was brought into the courtroom in handcuffs as I approached the bench and took a seat. Within the limited time period, I tried to enlighten the judge of the twenty-three years of marriage to Luke that had become unbearable for me. As I finished, the judge had Luke to come forward and give his account of the situation.

Luke said, "Well, Judge, I do construction work, and when the weather is bad, you know I can't work. When you don't *work*, them women at Western Electric don't want you 'round 'em!" He continued, "I hadn't been long gettin' out of drug treatment, and I am tryin' to get my life together!"

The judge asked, "Mr. Dunbar, where do you stay the entire weekends that you don't come home?"

"Yo' Honor, I be at LSU Hospital sleepin' on the benches in the admittin' room!"

The Judge wasn't buying Luke's *cockamamie crap*.

Luke's eyes bucked and his face frowned, "Judge, you mean to tell me that you gonna put me outta my own house?"

"Mr. Dunbar, you put yourself out. And I mean it. Don't you go back there again!" said the judge.

Luke was shocked! He was led out of the court room, yelling, "Where am I gonna stay? Man, that ain't right! Puttin' a man outta his own house!"

I was finally set free of my self-imposed sentence and what better way to make it official than by the court order. Of course, I knew that the judge had been used as an instrument, because God had the final word. I could not contain myself while driving down the interstate, yelling, "Yes! Yes!" repeatedly. I felt that I had been let out of my cell and given a reprieve. It was a fantastic feeling.

At home, I sat quietly in my favorite chair, trying to put all that had happened into perspective. I felt profoundly amazed at how last night's dream revealed itself to me. *That was my grandmother in my dream, and her sister, Nannie!* Mama's and Nannie's spirit were celebrating me finally getting rid of that "dry turnip."

I thought about Saturday, when Luke insisted on getting arrested. It was all working on my behalf. With that revelation, I was inspired with awe. I went into my bedroom and fell to my knees, crying joyful tears, saying, "Oh, thank you, Lord! Thank You! Thank You! Thank you!" I just couldn't thank Him enough! I was immediately reminded of that Bible verse in Roman 8:28, where it says that all things work together for the good of those who love the Lord, etc. The tears of joy overflowed, and I became humbly submissive to God.

The next morning when I returned to work, I was amazed again. Mysteriously, my pillar of strength and endurance, the one who had sat beside me all those months and been my moral support through my agony, was no longer there. Joyce had been moved farther down, to another position! She had completed the task that God had used her for.

Later, on my lunch break, I called the credit union inquiring about my loan approval. Because of poor credit history, and the fact that Luke would not be responsible for my bills any longer, my loan was denied.

I thought, *how preposterous! Luke is the primary reason for the poor credit history!* I pondered where I was going to get the means to pay the lawyer. With a feeling of utter dejection, I said within, "Lord! There always seems to be an obstacle thrown in my path."

Oops! Memory-lapse…God was still in control!

I returned to my work area and found another friend who knew about my situation waiting there for me.

Verna was her name. She was stout and witty. She always had something funny to say, and could make you laugh even on your worst days, but her heart was as generous as she was comical.

Verna asked, "Maple, you look disappointed. They didn't approve it?"

"No," I sighed heavily, "they said if I got a co-maker, they would approve it."

Smiling, Verna had a mischievous glint in her eyes, "I'll do it for you."

In surprise, I exclaimed, "Oh, no! You can't do that! I wouldn't even consider asking that of you!"

"Why not?" she asked, "We work at the same place and the money will automatically be deducted from your check weekly...not mine!" said Verna.

My eyes filled with tears as I grabbed and hugged her in gratitude.

Jokingly, Verna said, "Don't thank me yet! My credit might get rejected!" Of course, things worked out well.

Chapter 24
Mirroring his Environment

May 1988. At last, it was over...finished! No more stressful, roller coaster turbulent years with Luke. So I had thought, now I could get a grip on my life, and looked forward to having a sense of normalcy within my household. But what I didn't realize was that destructive behavior was the norm in our home, and my son, Jeff, had become a product of his environment, and mirrored that which he was exposed to.

My friend Joyce and I definitely had a special bond. I didn't realize the full extent of it, until a particular day, when she reluctantly approached me and said, "Maple, I had the strangest dream. I have been trying to decide whether or not to tell you."

"Joyce," I said, "you can tell me anything. Anyway, it was just a dream!"

She said, "I dreamed about Jeff. He was so high on drugs, he could barely hold his head up, and in a slurred voice he repeatedly cried for you. The dream really disturbed me. I had to pray about it, because I didn't want to tell you!"

"Don't feel bad," I told her, "because you have no control over what you dream."

I tried to make light of it, because I definitely knew Jeff would not involve himself in drugs, after seeing how they had affected his father. Jeff had more sense than to do drugs. But, the remainder of that day, I was somewhat apprehensive.

After getting home from work, I began doing the laundry. As always, I went into Jeff's room to see if there was any dirty laundry and got a shock. Beside his bed on the floor was an ashtray full of the funny looking cigarette butts, which were clearly marijuana. I cried out, "Oh my God! Joyce's dream wasn't *just* a dream!"

I dumped the remains of those terrible things in the trash and slumped down into my chair in despair. *Oh, Lord! What am I going to do now?* Later that night, Jeff came home.

"Jeff, I need to talk to you."

"What is it Mama?"

"I found an ashtray full of marijuana butts in your room."

Jeff gave me a blank stare.

"I'm so disappointed in you, Jeff." I continued, "How can you smoke that mess when you see what drugs are doing to yo' father!"

He remained silent, but he had a withdrawn and defiant look.

"Well, I'm tellin' you right now that I will not have drugs in *my* house! If you're going to do drugs, you *cannot* stay here!"

Jeff gave a nod, but he remained silent. I had thought that would be the end of that situation.

However, my life had been so consumed by Luke and Jeff's behavior, that I had somehow lost sight of Carl.

In the month of June, Jeff said, "Mama, I saw Carl in the mall with some boys, and they were the wrong type for him to be hanging with. You need to have a talk with him before he gets into trouble!"

Later that evening, I said, "Come here, Carl, and sit down in the living room. I need to talk with you."

Sixteen-year-old Carl, who had grown to a lanky six feet four inches, sat down on the couch, and I began to lecture him about the wrong associates and reminded him of his probation restriction of being at the mall without an adult chaperon.

Carl, who had never disrespected me, suddenly stood up and began mildly protesting. Then, as swift as lightning, Jeff, who stood about five feet eight inches and stoutly built, stormed into the room, grabbed Carl by his collar, and said angrily, "Little nigga, you think you're tough! You ain't tough! You keep hangin' around with them ole' thugs and see just where you end up! In trouble, that's where!" He continued, "You want to be bad? Then show *me* how bad you are!"

I stood momentarily shocked and baffled by Jeff's actions toward his brother. I said, "Jeff, what is the matter with you? Have you gone crazy? You don't treat Carl that way!"

Jeff said, "Mama, he needs a man to straighten him out!"

"That may be the case!" I said, "But you are not the one to straighten him out. You need straightening out yo'self!"

Jeff's sudden surge of anger disappeared and was replaced with a look of despair. As tears filled his eyes, he said in frustration, "Mama, somebody has got to make something out of their lives! This family is just pitiful! They're either in jail or on *dope*! Somebody ought to make *something* out of their life!"

"I agree. Someone should make something out of their life," I said. "So why can't you? It's not too late for you. You can be an example for Carl."

With the tears running down his cheeks, a silent Jeff, just shook his head. However, Carl had been secretly and quietly doing his own thing.

I carefully observed and inquired about his friends. I noticed he didn't seem to have any friends at church. He was a junior usher, but he didn't mingle with the others. I tried to encourage him to be more sociable but was unsuccessful. So, I dismissed his anti-social behavior as shyness because of his height. He was the tallest of his peers.

But, who was this tall boy about Carl's height and age, with the glassy red eyes, who suddenly started appearing at my door, looking for Carl? Perhaps it was my motherly intuition. I had an eerie feeling about this stranger.

"Carl," I questioned, "who is that boy and where does he live?"

"His name is Sean, Mama."

"Well, who are his people?"

"Why you askin' me all these questions about him? He's just a friend," answered an irritated Carl.

"Because I don't think you need him for a friend."

Carl's eyes bucked and he said, "Why you sayin' that? Do you know him?"

"No, I don't know him. But I don't have a good feeling about him, and you are not to be with him," I demanded.

I also put limitations on his recreational activities. He was restricted from going to the community's park, because he had broken his probation by going to the mall. I had thought that my rules and regulations were being carried out. But one Saturday, around one o'clock p.m., Carl received permission to go to our small neighborhood playground. At about 4 p.m., the telephone rang and I was informed that Carl was at the large community park, sick.

Alarmed, I drove to Airport Park, and found Carl inside the recreational building on the floor. He had regurgitated, was semi-conscious, and in a dazed condition with spectators surrounding him.

Oh, Lord! I thought, *what is wrong with my child? He must have fallen and hit his head on that floor!* As the lady assisted me to my car with Carl, she said, "I don't know exactly what happened to him. One minute I saw him shooting basketball, and the next minute I saw him lying sick on the floor!"

I drove fast to the hospital, trying desperately to avoid red lights, while Carl sat flopped in the seat with his head lying back on the headrest, protesting in a slurred voice, "I don't want to go to the hospital! I just want to go home and sleep!" said Carl.

"No!" I cried out, "I am taking you to the hospital, now! You're sick!"

The wheels of the car screeched to an abrupt halt when I parked it at the emergency entrance. I ran inside, frantically asking, "Would somebody please help me get my son out of the car. He's unconscious!"

The two nursing attendants hastily grabbed a gurney. Carl was placed into a room.

With trembling hands, I filled out the necessary papers, returned to the room where Carl was lying on the table, and was what I had thought him to be … unconscious.

The doctor finally appeared, examined Carl, and then asked what I thought was the most preposterous question to be asking a sixteen-year-old boy. "Son, have you been drinking?"

I was annoyed with that doctor. "My son doesn't drink," I snapped.

The doctor only nodded and continued examining Carl. Then he ordered a blood sample and urinalysis and quickly exited the room, only to return minutes later with a shocking report.

"Mrs. Dunbar, your son is drunk."

I stared at the doctor in disbelief and said, "No, you're mistaken! My son doesn't drink!"

"Your son has an alcohol level that is declared legally drunk."

"*WHAT?*" I shouted.

"I'm sorry, Mrs. Dunbar, but your son has gotten sick from drinking."

I slumped into the chair, devastated.

Carl admitted to drinking beer but couldn't remember how many he had consumed. Carl was dehydrated and was kept over night in the hospital.

I just knew that would be the end of Carl's drinking days. But the next weekend, after he was discharged from the hospital, I allowed him to go to a neighborhood party, and he returned with beer on his breath. I tried even more to be aware of Carl's activities and his associates.

Jeff told me he had seen Carl and Sean, his forbidden friend, at the liquor store together.

I began to notice Carl's red eyes but did not detect liquor on his breath. When I questioned Carl as to why his eyes were red, he said he had gotten something in them and he had been rubbing his eyes. And being my naïve self, I believed him.

In the meantime, Jeff had lost another job. All I required of him was that he maintained employment and reimburse me for his car payment. He had no other responsibility; Jeff was twenty-one years old and had free food and shelter. I was fed up with his irresponsible behavior. Before Jeff lost his job, he had gotten a $68 speeding ticket. He had supposedly paid the ticket, which meant no reimbursement for his car payment that month, and I understood.

***

A month later, Jeff was once again employed. However, that week I intercepted a telephone message from the deputy sheriff's office, reminding him of the ticket he said he had paid. Jeff had lied.

Therefore, I felt it was important to let him know I wasn't Mama the Fool any-more. I had graduated from that school of being used and didn't care to pursue that field of education any further. I had earned my degree for Naïvety and Dumbness with honors…all A's!

When Jeff came to me after receiving his first check, he said, "Mama, my check wasn't but $38. How much of it do you want?"

"I want thirty-dollars!"

"You want what?" He yelled.

"Thirty." I responded, firmly.

Jeff was shocked. "Man, I don't believe this! My check wasn't but $38, and you want to take it all but $8! Mama, you're wrong! You want to take *all* my money and that ain't right!"

"No! I'm not wrong!" I responded angrily, as I began to preach him another sermon about responsibility and lying about his ticket.

Jeff responded, "Well, I'm going to leave here!"

I called his bluff. "Help yourself." I said. "Because there is just too much arguing between us and you are getting very disrespectful!"

He reluctantly gave me the money, as he furiously shouted, "You're wrong! And I ain't gonna be givin' you all *my* money!"

I tried reasoning with Jeff, who wanted no part of it. He said angrily, "There ain't nothing to discuss. You want to take *all* my money!"

He was outraged, but I was determined to stand my ground. In the past, I would have given in to him, but not this time. I felt I was right, and I showed no mercy. I was trying to teach Jeff to become more responsible, and perhaps I went about it the wrong way.

Nevertheless, just when I was comfortable with the thought that I had dug through the only pile of rocks in the tunnel and could see clearly...not so! There was another pile waiting for me.

***

That next Thursday night, Jeff said, "Mama, I got paid today and my check wasn't but $65. I borrowed $3 and applied it to help pay my traffic ticket today. So I don't have any money to give you on the car payment."

"That's alright about the money Jeff, since you have paid your traffic ticket."

"Mama, will you give me $5 so that I can put gas in my car?"

"Sure!" I responded, "If you let me see the receipt where you paid your ticket."

Unfortunately, I threw fuel to the simmering coals and ignited the fire. Jeff's jaws dropped. He suddenly became enraged and yelled out angrily, "Why I got to let you see the receipt?"

My jaws dropped! I was startled, "Because you lied before about payin' this same ticket. I will not give you any money until I see the receipt!" I said.

Seeing that I was serious, he said, "I'll go to the car and get the receipt." Jeff went outside and returned about five minutes later and said to me, "I can't find the receipt. I guess I lost it."

Suspiciously, I questioned him about the receipt.

Suddenly Jeff became enraged. He shouted, "I don't have to let you see no receipt! I don't need yo' help or Daddy! That's all right. I'm gettin' outta here!"

Shocked, I thought, *Lord, what is wrong with Jeff? He has been acting irate lately.*

Jeff stormed into his room, slamming the door behind him. Then I heard an excessive amount of noise being made in his room. I went to investigate and found him packing his clothes.

"Are you leaving?" I asked Jeff.

"Yes!" he snapped, "I'm leaving here!"

"That's fine with me, Jeff." I snapped, "You leave. But the car stays here!"

Jeff responded, "That's *my* car, and you ain't takin' it!"

"You are not leaving here in that car!" I said, "You think I am going to allow you to run off to Dallas in a car that I'm paying for? Oh no! That car stays here! So you give me the keys to it, right now."

Jeff looked at me as if I was talking foolishness, and yelled, "You ain't *gettin'* no key. That's *my* car, and you ain't gettin' it. Last week, you took all my money. Now you want to take my car. Well, you ain't gettin' it!"

Jeff looked and spoke with hatred for me. His teeth were clenched tightly as if he was about to explode. At that point, I became cautious of my son. I was finally awakened to the fact that he wasn't a little boy, but a twenty-one-year old man. I tried reasoning with him, to no avail. I threatened to call the police.

He yelled, "Call the police! You still ain't gonna get my car!" He was pacing back and forth, mumbling and muttering low, indistinct words, doing a copycat of Luke's erratic behavior.

I hurriedly phoned Luke, hoping he would talk to Jeff. After I explained the situation, Luke agreed. But Jeff would not cooperate and yelled out loudly, *"I don't need you and I don't need him!"*

Wearily I said to Luke, "Jeff is acting strange! If he doesn't calm down and give me those keys, I will have to call the police on him!"

Luke suddenly became hostile. "Yeah, you call the police! You know you're good at that!" he snapped.

Now ain't that some shit!

In the meantime, Jeff had taken his suitcase to the car. When he came back into the house, I confronted him calmly and firmly, "Jeff, I mean it. Don't leave here in that car."

Jeff stormed into his room for a second time, slammed the door and began throwing objects, hitting the wall with his fist and kicking the door.

My tolerance had reached its limit. Blinded by anger, I opened the door to Jeff room, it was a disaster. I got into his face and yelled, *"Boy! What is yo' problem?"*

Jeff did not respond as the tears streamed down his face.

As I glanced around that room, I wanted to "snatch a knot" in Jeff's ass.

"Yes!" I said, "You go! But that car stays here and I want the keys, right now!"

Jeff glared at me and walked swiftly pass me into the living room with me right at his heels. He spoke in a cold and definite tone. "I ain't got the keys, and you *better* stay away from me, Mama. Cause I ain't gonna let you hurt me!"

After hearing Jeff speak those words, Carl, who had remained in his room throughout the ordeal suddenly emerged and said, "Mama, let that fool alone! You see that he's actin' crazy!"

"Go back into yo' room," I commanded Carl. "I'll handle this!"

Carl stood there, looking uncertain and repeated himself. I assured him I could handle it. Carl hesitated but returned to his room.

"Jeff," I said, "I have no intention of hurting you! All I want from you are those car keys!"

He refused.

I was in a dilemma and struggled inwardly. *Why don't I just surrender and let him have that car? On the other hand, if I allow him to get his way with this, in the future it would become even worse. No way! I am not giving in to him. Not this time!*

But, I gave a plea. "Son, you leave me no other choice but to call the police if you leave here in that car!"

"Go ahead!" Jeff snapped, "Call them, cause you ain't gettin' my car!"

Reluctantly, I telephoned the police as Jeff looked in disbelief. He suddenly ran out of the house. The car remained parked, but Jeff had disappeared.

I slumped into my chair in agony, hoping and wishing that the whole scene had been a nightmare and I would awake.

Two policemen finally arrived. I asked them not to arrest Jeff, only talk some sense into him.

They waited patiently for Jeff to return, but he never did. Before leaving they suggested that if I decided to allow Jeff to take the car, I needed to keep the ownership papers.

I had no intentions of allowing Jeff to drive off with that car. I remembered the extra set of keys and I summoned Carl's help. We switched the cars, and I removed the ownership papers from the car. Not long afterward, Jeff returned.

"Mama!" said Jeff, "you *better* move yo' car from behind mine!"

That word "better" struck a nerve with me. I asked, "What did you say Jeff?"

"You heard me, and I ain't playin'! You had *better* move yo' car, if you don't, then I will move it for you."

Outraged, I moved toward him and said coldly, "Who in the *hell* do you think that you are talkin' to? Boy! I will kill you!" I threatened, as my grandmother's strength and character sprung up in me.

Jeff's ball-fisted hands were stiffly down at both his sides, as if he was in an attack mode, and he had a fierce look. He again said, "Mama, you had *better* move yo' car from behind mine. If you don't, I'll back over it!"

Again, I thought, *Lord, this has got to be a nightmare. This is not my son talking to me this way!*

I tried again to reason with Jeff.

He yelled, "I don't want to talk to you. I don't want to have anything else to do with you. Furthermore, you ain't my mama! I don't have no Mama!" He returned to his room, and again went on a rampage for the third time. I could hear him hitting the walls with his fist and uttering profanity.

My eyes flashed on Jeff's baseball bat standing against the wall in the hallway. Hoping to intimidate Jeff with the bat, but not to physically do harm to my son, I grabbed it and I ran into his room, "Jeff, I've had enough! You get out of here before something drastic happens between us!"

"I ain't going no where, until I get my car." Jeff growled.

I could see the violence in Jeff's eyes, as I had no doubt whatsoever that he would forcefully attempt to get that car. I became distressed, as all the energy left my body. The baseball bat dropped from my hand. I had no fight left.

I sighed heavily and made the most ridiculous statement. "Jeff," I said, "you can take that car, providing you don't leave town, running back to Dallas in it! And I expect to be paid every week!" I continued, "But you can't stay here anymore!"

Jeff responded, "I don't want to stay with you, and I ain't going to Dallas to live!"

I informed Jeff that I was keeping the registration papers and that brought about another confrontation. He refused to leave without those papers. I refused to give them to him, and he left the house, walking.

I flopped down in my recliner, and I wanted to scream, but I was numb. I said within, *When Jeff returns, he can definitely have those papers and get the hell out of my life!* I went and removed my car from behind his. Minutes later, Jeff returned.

"Here are the papers." I said, "But, if you leave town in that car I will have an arrest warrant served on you!"

He took the papers and was about to get into his car; however, those same two policemen pulled up and commanded that he come into the house. We all sat down in the living room and they had a conference with Jeff. They reminded him of me being the legal owner of the car and even suggested that he apologize to me.

Jeff, who was still on probation from his previous trouble, remained hostile, and belligerent to the point where one of the officers threatened to place him under arrest.

Jeff said to the officers, "You can put me in jail cause I ain't gonna apologize to her! I don't want to have anything else to do with her!"

One of the officers quickly jumped up and started toward Jeff, as if he wanted to shake some sense into him.

Then, in spite of it all, my motherly love and instinct caused me to intervene. I said, "Jeff, they don't want to take you to jail. They only want you to calm down!"

Jeff shouted out, *"I don't want you sayin' anything to me!"*

Weary, defeated, and surrendering, I said to the officers, "Let him go! Just let him get out of my sight!"

"Ma'am, if you are going to allow him to have that car, you need to go and get a copy of the registration papers. You keep the original ones and give him the copy," said the concerned officer.

Jeff reluctantly relinquished the papers, and I told him to come back tomorrow, and I would have his copy. Then the officers watched Jeff to make sure that he left and that I was safe. Carl, who had remained silent throughout the police involvement, shook his head and went into his room. I was left alone with my grief.

My mind didn't want to digest what had actually occurred. It was inconceivable. My son that I birthed, loved, nurtured, made many sacrifices for, tried to teach him moral values and tried to plant that spiritual "seed" in him at a very young age, would destroy and tear my heart into tiny pieces. I felt an incredible pain in my chest. The pain stung as if hundreds of pins jabbed my heart. And my heart felt as if it was being ripped out of my chest. It was too much to bear!

I went into my bedroom and fell to my knees, trying to pray, but words failed me and my tears were blocked behind a brick wall. In agony, I could only utter, "Oh, Lord!" repeatedly. I remained on my knees with my face buried in the bed. Finally, with a lifeless body, I struggled into bed and spent a restless, tormented night.

Friday morning, I gathered enough strength to get out of bed and went to work in a dazed condition. When I entered the plant, my body wanted to crumble to the floor. I cried, "Oh, God, dear God. How can I do my job today? I don't think I can make it."

"Yes, you can," answered a whispering voice.

"But, God, my heart is so broken. And my mind is so confused."

"I know," said the voice, "but you are stronger than you know."

"But God, I need your help!"

"I'm here. Lean on me," said the voice.

I tried to immerse myself into my work. I was glad Joyce no longer sat beside me. The conflict between Jeff and me was just too humiliating to share, even with her. Yet, a co-worker seated across from me brought me back into my painful world. "Maple, you have such a strange look on your face. Are you alright?"

"Yes," I mumbled, "I'm OK."

But I wasn't. At that moment I felt like running through the plant screaming, wailing and tearing at my flesh. But, I knew if that happened, it would have been the end of me as I had known me to be.

That was the darkest day of my life. Several times, I gasped outwardly in agony and muttered, "Oh, Lord! Please see me through this day!"

Whenever a distressful feeling came over me the voice would speak to me saying repeatedly, "You must be strong, now! You cannot fold under! You must not give in!"

I found myself silently repeating different passages of Bible verses and singing two old gospel hymns: *Father, I stretch my hands to thee; No other help I know; If thou withdraw thyself from me, Ah, whither shall I go?* The other: *I love the Lord: he heard my cries, and pitied every groan: Long as I live, when troubles rise, I'll hasten to his throne.* I sang those over and over in my head. In my youth I had thought of those old dragging hymns as out of date ... not realizing their powerful message. But now, they were my lifelines used as a vessel to hold on to my sanity.

My heart was so thankful for my grandmother who had taught me to pray, and insisted that I go to Sunday school, church, and read my Bible during my childhood, and for the other Christian relatives who had helped nourish me in the knowledge of the Lord. I had acquired and reached from the past a source of strength that I had never before used...God's sustaining grace and power! I was fragile, torn, and broken-hearted, but by the end of that workday, I had persevered. Oh, thanks be to God whose grace is sufficient!

On my way home, I stopped and made a copy of those papers for Jeff. About thirty minutes later, he came by and said coldly, "I came for the papers," as he avoided making eye contact.I gave him the papers and reminded him of his obligations…no desertion and weekly payment.

Jeff would not look me in the eyes. He said, "I told you, I'm gonna pay you, and I am not leavin' town." Having spoken those words, Jeff got into his car and never looked back.

That night, I knelt down again to pray, but was too distressed. I tossed and turned throughout the night, repeating those same two words, "Oh, Lord!" and asking myself, "What have I done to deserve this?" Before daybreak, my mind was in such turmoil I became petrified, and felt I had to get beyond my cries of "Oh, Lord!" I knew there was an emotional outburst, still behind that brick wall that was bottled up inside of me that had to be released. Psalm 30:6 says "weeping may endure for a night, but joy cometh in the morning." I didn't know what the exact Biblical time-frame "in the morning" was determined on. So, I tried to hold it together, and wait on *that joy.*

However, in many sermons, I'd heard ministers' say, "Allow me to use my sanctified imagination."

But, my not having had a sanctified imagination, rather a carnal mind, between the hour of 4:00 and 5:00 a.m., in my carnal imagination, all I could see was C-R-A-Z-Y! A voice spoke to me, saying, "If you don't do something, and do it quickly...you're going to lose it! You need *help*!"

"Joyce!" I cried, "I'm so sorry to call you at this hour of the morning, but I need to talk with you!"

"Maple." she asked in a drowsy voice, "What is the matter?"

As I talked, my eyes flooded and tears streamed down my face.

"You want me to ask my husband to come to the phone and pray for you?" she asked.

"Please do!" I answered.

Joyce's husband was on the telephone immediately. His deep, strong, preacher's voice was interceding to God, praying, "Oh Father, whatever is troubling her, please give her a peace of mind." The reverend petitioned God on my behalf, and with each sentence spoken, the brick wall loosened and fell away, brick by brick. THANK GOD FOR THE PREACHER!

I fell to my knees and could finally let go of those emotions. It was an eruption of tears and sobs. Then I prayed.

***

All of that next week I tried to stay focused on my work and remain sane, but I felt my heart was bleeding, and there wasn't a bandage large enough to stop the blood. However, that Friday Jeff never showed up. I waited anxiously all weekend, hoping that my intuition would prove me wrong. But, by that Sunday night, I felt it was time for me to come out of that "bleeding heart" syndrome. I was determined to get well and get busy.

Monday morning, after making inquiries and finding a Dallas telephone number on a previous bill, my suspicion was proven true; Jeff had run off to Dallas! I left Jeff a message with the reluctantly co-operative girl who answered the telephone.

Later that day, Jeff phoned. "Mama, I heard that you were looking for me."

"Yes!" I said, "It is obvious that you don't take me seriously concerning that car! So I guess I will have to prove to you that I am serious!"

Jeff said angrily, "That's my car, and you ain't gonna get it! You can just forget that you have a son, because I ain't never comin' back there, any more!"

Click.

***

Three weeks had gone by with the car still being in Jeff's possession. After much deliberation, I knew that my salary would not allow me to continue paying two car payments. That Saturday in September, the weekend before Labor Day, the time had arrived for Jeff to use what God had given him for transportation... his feet!

With the help of Luke and another man, we left Shreveport about 6 a.m. and drove to Dallas. At approximately 10 a.m., we found the car in this apartment complex parking lot, and Luke drove it back to Shreveport. Later that evening, Jeff phoned, making threats and giving me unwanted information about Luke's liaisons. But, that next week, I was given some information about Jeff that left me mentally distressed and wanting to scream, *"Oh, No! Not Jeff!"* I was told that Jeff had used cocaine. I didn't know whether it was factual, or not. But, that seemed to shed some light on his irate and bizarre behavior.

***

For over a month, the little red Subaru had been parked in front of the house with a For Sale sign on it. Late that November evening, I answered the knock at the door, and there was Jeff. I opened the door and allowed him to come inside. He had a sad look on his face, and said, "Mama, I'm sorry for the way that I acted. Can I come back home?"

Without hesitating I responded, "I accept your apology, Jeff. But, I'm sorry, you can't stay here any more!"

Jeff looked stunned and asked, "Where am I going to stay if I can't stay with you?"

"I don't know." I answered, "That's your problem. When you were here, we were always in conflict, with you either leaving or threatening to leave. Now that you are out there, you will have to make it on your own!" I spoke firmly.

Jeff left his nest with a dejected look on his face.

I had no second thoughts about my decision. I didn't trust Jeff. I felt that Jeff had ulterior motives, which were to eventually persuade me into giving him back the car, without any behavior improvement. I felt Jeff was not ready to come back home. I don't know to this day whether or not that was the right decision. I sometimes wonder "what if", but that decision is something I will have to live with.

***

In January 1989, Jeff turned twenty-two years of age, he had returned to Dallas, and eventually got arrested again, and was sentenced to three years in the penitentiary.

As it turned out, I had to take on a second job before I eventually sold that little red Subaru that had been the center of so much pain.

Chapter 25
Contaminating our Fruits

October of 1988: The remnant of my household had been reduced to just Carl and me, although Carl, who now was in the tenth grade, had been having his difficulties, I felt that he didn't present that much of a problem that I couldn't get a handle on. However, a seed from that negative environment had been planted in him. The fruit from that seed had grown to contaminate him.

"Mrs. Dunbar," said the lady, "this is the school administrative office. Your son Carl has acted in a very disrespectful manner with one of his teachers."

"What did he do?" I asked.

"He told his general business teacher to quote, unquote, "Fuck you!"

My mouth opened so wide, a freight train could have gone through it...SHOCKED!

"No, he didn't!"

"Yes, Mrs. Dunbar. We don't want to suspend him, but he needs to be reprimanded. And we noticed on his files that you had especially requested that if we should have any problems with him to contact you."

"Yes, I did." I said, "And I appreciate you for doing just that. I assure you I will get this matter taken care of immediately."

"We didn't tell him that we were going to contact you." said the lady.

"That's fine. We'll surprise him." I said, "I'm on my way!"

I left work, made a pit stop home, and off to the school I drove. I thought, *What's wrong with that boy? I'm not tolerating that type of behavior from Carl....having people thinking his Mama hadn't taught him to respect his elders! Back in the day, I would have been punished by my teacher and skinned alive by my grandmama! Oh no! Carl has gone too far!*

In the administration office, Carl's principal looked at me, puzzled. He shook his head saying, "Mrs. Dunbar, I don't understand why Carl would react that way by his teacher. She's a very sweet lady, who tries to teach students business, having them balance a check book and other requirements that they are going to need in managing the financial aspects of life." He continued, "The teacher is very upset and hurt by his comment."

My jaws tightened in fury. I said, "Will you have Carl to come to the office, please?"

The principal nodded and called Carl's classroom.

"When he gets here," I said, "will you step out of the office so that I can discipline him?"

The principal was taken aback. He said, "Well Mrs. Dunbar, that is against school policy. However, in this case I will allow it."

The principal walked out when Carl walked in. Seeing me, Carl's eyes bucked. "What you doin' here, Mama?" asked Carl.

"I was called about your behavior and the word that you used to yo' teacher is outrageous!" I snapped, "Boy, what's wrong with you? You know better than to say something like that!"

"Mama, that old teacher just don't like me!" said Carl, "and she gets on my nerves!"

"Gets on yo' nerves!" I repeated. "Well, I'm gonna get on more than yo' nerves."

I could hear from the next room, those whispering voices of the staff members saying, "shh" as I went into my purse and brought out my big leather belt.

Carl's eyes bucked and his mouth flew opened. "Mama!" cried Carl, "Why you comin' up here trippin'? I know you ain't gon' whip me here!"

"Oh yes I am."

I mustered all the strength I had and applied punishment to his sixteen-year-old, six-foot four-inch body. I preached a sermon with every lash. With the last lash, I warned, "If I have to come again because of yo' bad behavior, you will be punished in yo' classroom, where the other students will see!"

Carl, with tears running down his cheeks, nodded his head in silence.

I walked out into the administrative staff's office and offered an apology for my disturbance. One staff member said, "Mrs. Dunbar, we wish many more parents were like you."

Acting all pious, with my head held up high in the air, I felt that I had made my point; I was a mother that would let it be known that Carl wasn't raised in that manner. I didn't realize that Carl was only mirroring what he had grown up with. Carl was just a product of the environment that his parents had created. *Flashback!* In Carl's mind, money and "fuck you" belonged together like "peas and carrots!"

My landlord, Reverend Townsel's sudden, and untimely death brought about a change in our residence. His wife, Mrs. Townsel, generously offered me a hand up by allowing me to continue live in her home three months, rent free. That helped me to have enough funds to make a deposit on an apartment, and to pay the cost of moving expenses. (God bless Mrs. Townsel!)

***

In March of 1989, Carl and I moved to a very nice apartment complex, farther out west of Shreveport on West 70th Street, in a totally different surrounding, and I had thought that our future was going to shine as bright as that sunny day that we had moved. But, just as soon as I had emerged out of the murky miry clay and was trying to set my feet on solid ground, in a wink, I was quickly immersed back into the clay.

That summer, Carl, now seventeen-years-old, got a part-time job within walking distance from home. I was proud of him. He was still active in church as a junior usher and seemingly life was looking up for a change. It was going to be a calm, peaceful, and beautiful summer.

However, Carl, I noticed often left home in one condition and came home in another. I could detect the smell of beer on his breath. It was obvious he had been drinking, especially on Friday nights.

When confronted, Carl denied that it was beer I smelled. Of course, all things considered I wasn't the naïve fool that I had once been. I laid down the law …no drinking! But, that next Friday the law meant absolutely nothing to Carl.

"Mama", said Carl, "I only had *one* beer!"

Carl never adhered to my three warnings, and his condition worsened. Out of fear, I took drastic measures and beat Carl with the broom. I reacted like a crazy person, and the punishment proved fruitless. The next Friday night when Carl came home, he could not stand up straight, reeling and rocking in a drunken state.

Alarmed, I remembered the oil ritual. I thought, *if that oil worked on Luke, it would work on Carl!* I ran into my bedroom, grabbed that bottle of sacred oil which was kept in a secret place and returned to Carl's room.

Carl was sitting on his bed, looked up at me with a frightening gaze. "Mama what you fixin' to do?"

"I'm going to anoint yo' head with this *oil* and get that *demon* outta you!"

Carl's eyes were about to pop out!

I applied the oil to his forehead and commanded, "Satan, I rebuke you in the name of Jesus. *Come outta my child*!" Carl sat frozen, afraid to move. He was staring at me like I was a lunatic!

If my bed pillow had had life, it would have been squeezed to death as I clung to it, fell to my knees at the foot of my bed, rocking back and forth, sobbing and pleading, "Please, God! Oh please save my child! Save my child, Lord. Please save my child!"

Saturday morning, I arose early. Ironically, my irrational behavior had caused Carl to do something that he had never done before...he had locked his door! However, he allowed me to enter.

Grasping for understanding, I asked, "Carl, why are you drinking?"

Looking sad, Carl shook his head. "I don't know, Mama."

"Am I the cause of you drinking, Carl?"

"No, Mama!"

"Well, why?"

"I don't know!" Carl exclaimed.

"Carl, there has to be a reason for your drinking. If it is me, then tell me!"

Carl looked puzzled and said, "Mama, *I just don't know!*"

My eyes filled with tears as a feeling of despair came upon me. I said, "Carl, if you come home again and have been drinking, I will have to get you some help!"

Carl nodded his head in agreement.

Frankly, I thought my threat of getting help for Carl would put an end to his drinking. I never felt it would come to that extreme. But, that next Friday night, Carl appeared worse than ever before.

Monday, I called and made an appointment for Carl at a local treatment center for that following Saturday.

Carl protested and promised; no more drinking. That next Friday night, Carl was sober. But I was not going to allow that to become a factor in my decision. Saturday morning we kept our appointment.

We arrived at the treatment center and were interviewed by a female administrator. After I gave her a short background history of addiction that had been in the family, she interviewed Carl privately.

For about thirty minutes I sat there in the main lobby. Finally, as I entered the room, I looked at Carl. He had tears in his eyes, and his head bowed when the lady said, "Mrs. Dunbar, Carl told me that he has been drinking off and on for about two years."

My heart pounded, and my body became weak as I got this empty feeling in the pit of my stomach.

"Not only has he been drinking," she continued, "but he has been using marijuana too."

I looked over at Carl, and a dull aching pain emerged in my heart. I wanted to scream out, "*Oh no! Not you, too!*" I cried, "Oh, Lord! My baby!"

Carl looked over at me with teary eyes. The tears began swelling in my eyes as I fought to maintain my composure.

The lady continued, "Mrs. Dunbar, don't get alarmed. Most teenagers nowadays are experimenting with alcohol and marijuana. It is nothing uncommon. However, with it being an addiction in your family's history, we would like to keep Carl for a week of observation. However, within that week, Carl cannot have outside contact with anyone, not even you, Mrs. Dunbar."

I looked over at Carl, and a big lump formed in my throat. I fought the impulse to grab my son and hold him close to me. I felt so sorry for him. I wanted to fix the problem and protect him from whatever he was about to face, but I knew that this, too, was something that I couldn't fix. It was out of my control! I said to Carl as he looked at me for reassurance, "It's going to be alright, Carl!"

Carl fought to keep the tears from his eyes.

After making arrangements and completing the admission form, I returned home and packed Carl enough clothes for his week's stay at the center, while thinking what a gullible fool I'd been. Just when I thought that I was a wiser person to the things that were going on around me, I discovered that I was still in my "shoe box" and had only gotten half way out. But, that's all right! I was so thankful that I got Carl to the treatment center, just in time! He would realize within that week that what he has been doing is hazardous and afterwards he would be back with me and everything hereafter was going to be alright!

I returned to the center with Carl's clothes. After giving him a kiss goodbye, with great expectations, I left my son there. Throughout the next week, I kept a positive attitude. I felt that during that week everything would be wrapped up in a neat little package and knew Carl would be coming back home with me.

***

On an August Saturday morning, I arrived at the center for my 9 a.m. appointment. Parents and patients were shown a film about chemical dependency. Afterwards, everybody introduced themselves, with the patients being named specifically. When it was Carl's time, I wasn't prepared when he said, "My name is Carl. I'm an alcoholic."

I gasped in shock as the energy left my body. Astounded, I slumped back into the chair and wanted to cry out, *No! No! You're not an alcoholic! I got you here in time!* In agonizing desperation, I cried inwardly, "Oh, Lord! Have Mercy!" I knew then that my son was not returning home with me.

I was numb and dazed while getting instructions on family members' participation. Afterwards, I drove home and sat down in that old chair and wept. "Why?" I questioned God. "Where have I gone wrong?" I remembered the incident when Jeff had said in frustration, "Mama, somebody ought to make somethin' out of their life. This family is just pitiful! They're either in jail or on dope!"

I thought, *Oh, Lord! It's true!* Luke's brothers were either in jail or on drugs, as was Luke. Jeff was incarcerated. Now Carl announced that he is an alcoholic! Weeping, I asked, "God! Will there ever be any *good* to come out of *this* family?"

***

September 1989: For those thirty days that Carl was in treatment, I participated fully. However, I noticed that at the family group sessions, Carl would never participate, and his eyes would never make contact with mine. Carl never let his inner feelings be known to me. I also attended the after-care programs for family members. I listened to all the horrific stories of family members' addictions and relapses. In all candor, I attended those meetings but I never really got the scope of it, the magnitude. It was as if I was there, but I wasn't there. Perhaps it was because I was still carrying the residue from all that had previously happened in my life, and that I just wasn't ready to digest it all. Or perhaps I was still in a stage of denial because I actually thought that Carl didn't really have a problem and after his treatment he would be walking the straight and narrow.

In that third week of September, the soon to be eighteen-year-old Carl was released from the treatment center. He was to have follow-ups with the aftercare program. Carl attended a few meetings, after which he decided not to continue. I insisted upon him continuing, but I somehow failed in my efforts. However, he did re-enroll in school. He was also fortunate enough to get his part-time job back.

I was very optimistic and knew that I had definitely crawled and clawed my way to the light at the end of this tunnel. But I was, as usual, deluding myself.

1 Peter 5:8 says: "Be sober and be vigilant; because your adversary the devil, as a roaring lion, walketh about, seeking whom he may devour." That verse seemed to apply to my family. We were being picked, plucked, and torn apart!

To my dismay, Carl, who had only been back into the school system about a month, began behaving worse than ever before. First, he was suspended for fighting. Three days later, we were in the principal's office in conference. Afterward, Carl was readmitted.

One definite lesson that I had learned while participating in the treatment program, my punishment of whippings was no longer feasible. But I still, lectured Carl and expected him to abide by the rules of the house, and he was definitely going to get that high school diploma. I was not going to have another dropout. He must attend church and there would be no drinking or drug use. My efforts were for naught. Carl made three new friends at school. They were also troublemakers and were suspected of gang affiliation. After having been readmitted to school after that first suspension, Carl was suspended a second time within a month…for fighting again!

Carl's behavior really put that principal to the test. He had reached his limit and was not tolerating Carl any longer. However, he really tried to reach Carl one last time, "Son, don't you see where your actions are heading?" he pleaded. "Stop this self-destructive pattern before it's too late!" But Carl continued to look defiant.

That same evening, I ran an errand, and upon returning to the apartment complex I found Carl handcuffed, inside a police car, under arrest. He and those same three boys from school had attacked a boy that lived in the apartment complex. The motherly Black lady officer took it upon herself to try to reach-out to Carl. She also pleaded with him to stop his destructive behavior. Carl was held in detention for several hours and was released. As a result of his second lawbreaking incident, he was put on six months probation.

The week following Carl's arrest, I accompanied him to enroll in the school's alternative program. The principal of that school was also very concerned and counseled with Carl. But all those frustrating years Carl had witnessed his parents "acting a fool" before him; the cursing, the fighting, all that negative destructive behavior that had been thrust upon him, which he had no control over. But the seed of contamination had been planted and lay dormant, waiting for its time to spring up. Now, my once quiet and sweet baby-boy, Carl, was on a destructive path and nothing said or done made a difference in his behavior.

***

After months of frustration, I fell to my knees, without emotions or tears. I was just simply worn out, dragged through the mud, body-weary and mind-weary, exhausted. I prayed, "God, I have done all I know to do. I have whipped. I have talked. I have gotten him some help through treatment. Others have talked to him and nothing seems to have made a difference. Now Lord, It is up to you! Carl is in your hands. Whatever it takes for him to listen- let it be!"

***

January 9, 1990: It had only been two weeks since I prayed that prayer. Now Carl had been arrested for murder.

Sitting there in my favorite chair, I took a journey back into the forty-five years of my life. I must have been sitting for over an hour, because the news reporter was again reporting the same news, *"Last night, at about 11 p.m., an attempted murder was committed during an attempted armed robbery and an eighteen-year-old black male suspect whose name is Carl Dunbar..."*

I had to get to the police station, but I didn't want to go. I wanted to just sit and sit in this big old ragged patched chair. It was reminiscent of the condition my life had been in...torn, worn out and ragged. And I just keep patching over it.

I got in my car, put my key into the ignition switch, started my car, when suddenly a light switch was turned on … and my dead heart came back to life. *Attempted murder! That's what the reporter said. Not murder! She didn't say murder! There's hope. The person is not dead.* My heart beat wildly. I cried out, "Oh, God, please don't let him die! Please don't let him die!"

At the police station, I was greeted by a black detective. She said, "Mrs. Dunbar, we have Carl's statement. We don't believe he actually committed the crime, but we caught your son and the others got away. Carl has been very cooperative."

I could feel energy come back into my limp body, and the tears that I was fighting to hold back began to flow. Barely a whisper, I said, "Thank you Lord, my son didn't commit this terrible crime!"

I asked, "Is the victim still alive?"

"Yes," she said, "and he was able to identify his attacker."

"Oh, thank you Jesus!" I said, as the burden of despair lifted.

The lady detective said that around 11 p.m., Carl and three other boys happened to see a man using an automated teller machine. One of the boys attempted to rob the man at gunpoint, but the man resisted, grabbed the gun, and was shot in the struggle. All the boys ran away, however Carl was apprehended.

The detective said, "Carl is a very lucky young man because the man could have been killed and he could have been charged with the crime."

My heart began to pound rapidly from her last words. With despair in my voice, I said to her, "I'm not surprised that Carl has gotten in trouble, because I have been talking to him and he hasn't been listening. I put him in the Lord's hands two weeks ago 'cause I had done all that I knew to do, and I failed."

"Mrs. Dunbar," said the detective, "it is not your fault if you know you've done all that you know how to do in bringing your child up in the right way. With today's kids it is just hard. I have a ten-year-old, and who knows? In another four or five years, or perhaps sooner, I may be on the other side of this desk about him, as you are today."

I could see the empathy in her eyes and felt her sincerity. I asked, "How long will he be in jail?"

"I don't know," she answered, "but it shouldn't be too long. You can come and visit him tomorrow at 4 o'clock." Carl was detained for two months before he was cleared of all charges.

I had actually thought that with Carl having had that experience, it would bring about a change in his behavior. It did, unfortunately, for the worse. With every fiber of my being, I tried to make Carl stay in school, but he also dropped out. Within a period of two years, Carl's life took a downward spiral that drained me mentally and physically, until I was at my wit's end. I just didn't know of anything else I could do, until that particular morning.

I can't remember exactly what reason I had for calling out Carl's name while simultaneously opening the door to his bedroom. But I did. And I was startled.

Carl, looking guilty, said, "Mama, it ain't what you think."

"Son, you have a gun, and crack cocaine in yo' possession. I don't hafta' think. I know!"

"But Mama, let me explain!"

"There's no explanation needed." I said, "Son, you got to get out!"

Carl had been sitting on his bed, stood up and towered over me. "Mama," he asked, "how can you put yo' own son out?"

A feeling of emptiness consumed me as I said, "Carl, I've done all I could do to help you. But *this*, I am not going to tolerate. You can't live under the same roof with me and be involved in drug activities." I stood firm, and said, "Son, I mean it. You got to go!"

On that particular day, I could have looked the other way and lived in a state of denial. That day, I could have chosen to become engaged in being an enabler. But, instead I chose to take a stand.

Therefore, in that year of 1992, Carl, at age twenty-one, was put out from my presence, but not from my heart.

***

After months of being on his own, then consequently living with Luke, in an environment that wasn't conducive, Carl decided he was ready to make a change in his life. And I was there for him. He enrolled in the Job Corp, twice, locally and out of State, but unfortunately, neither worked out for him. Thereafter, Carl's life has been a revolving door to the prison system, and so has Jeff's. *My worst fear became my reality.*

The year of 2010: both my sons are incarcerated at the same institution. They have spent the majority of their adult lives institutionalized. However, they are in the Work Release Program, and that gives me a glimmer of *hope*! Hope, that upon their release, they will have come to appreciate those hours of being productive citizens of this free country that we live in. Hope that they will continue on the path of freedom and making right choices. Hope that their future will shine bright and their lives will have meaning. *I have hope.*

Letter to My Sons

Listen, Sons, please listen...

Because of the choices you've made, your lives have not been productive. I now realize that I can't exclude myself for being a contributor to those bad choices. As parents, the foundation we laid before you were not built on a solid base. It had many cracks in it. At the time, I didn't fully grasp how home environment plays the most essential part of one's childhood. I was cognizant to some degree of the negativity of your father's and my destructive behavior before the two of you. But I never realized the magnitude of the effect it had on the development of your character. I thought that if you were brought up in the church, your lives would automatically turn out okay. But you were exposed to all the negative inappropriate behavior displayed between parents that should not have been. Having learned that children mirror what they are exposed to, I know why you both acted-out in your classrooms...there were so much chaos at home. It was never my intention to contaminate your childhood with those bad examples that we set before you. My desire was to raise happy sons, which would grow up to become productive, Christian men. But somewhere I lost sight of that. I realize now, my staying in a destructive marriage was not conducive for either of your development. I made many mistakes in my parenting, and I asked your forgiveness. Being your mother, it's too late for me to change those past mistakes, but it not too late for you. Sons, please don't continue allowing your past to determine the rest of your future. My sons, you have the intelligence and capability of sealing up those cracks. By turning your lives around, you can say goodbye to that past and hello to a brighter future. I hope I live to see that day. *My Sons, I'm praying for you!*

Meditation

Listen, Lord, please listen...

Forgive me for raising my sons in a hostile, negative, destructive environment.

Lord, I now realize that I did not do the best that I could have done by my sons. But at that time, I did the best that I knew how.

Forgive me for whatever mistakes I've made...please God.

Oh God, dear God who created my sons, please help my blind, misguided sons. Please open-up their eyes to freedom.

Oh, God, please give my sons some direction in their lives. Help them to become somebody other than career criminals. Help them to have pride in themselves. Give them goals to strive for. Help them to see that it is not too late to make something of their lives.

Please God, don't give them over to a reprobate mind. Instead, catch them by the reins of their mind.

Oh God, save their souls. Please don't let their souls be lost! Let your almighty wisdom grasp their intelligence before it's too late.

And God, I will surely give You the praise and the glory.

Now Lord. It's time to give thanks ...

Thank you, God, my sons are alive.

Thank you, God. Thank you for bringing me through those turbulent years.

God if it had not been for your grace and mercy, oh where would I be?

God, thank you for putting those special people in my life that helped to nurture my Christian growth. Oh, thank you God. You give your children what we need ... when we need it!

Thank you, God. Oh dear God how I thank you, for bringing peace in my life.

God, oh God, Thank you for your mercy. Every day a brand new mercy!

Thank you, God, for a mind…a healthy mind.

When I think about those dark days of despair, I can't help but to rejoice.

Thank you, God. Having come "through" all those trials and tribulations I am a much stronger person. I have evolved and developed into a character of strength beyond my wildest imagination.

God, oh how I thank you.Whenever I reflect over my life, it has been an incredible journey. And it's sometimes hard to believe I am that same person now as back then. But God, I believe You allow things to happen to us. Then You bring us out so that *You* can be glorified!

TO GOD BE THE GLORY

Epilogue

In the year 2000, Carl, my younger incarcerated son, who was twenty-nine years of age wrote me a four-page letter. He even gave it a title, "Reason: My true feelings!"

"To Momma: I know that you might not want to read what I'm about to write, but I'm going to write it anyway because it's been on my heart for years and it's time for it to come out. First of all, I know that I'm not the child that you want me to be, but I didn't ask to be here on this earth. God blessed you to have me here, and I thank him for that. I was born from a drug addicted father that have had drug problem throughout his life that runs in his family. I have a lot of his ways, from lying to mistreating people. He wasn't there for me or for Jeff as we were coming up, and that hurt my heart dearly because the father is supposed to be the head of the house. I felt like he didn't care about me at all. You was there for me because you had no choice. Yes, you taught me a lot of things but you couldn't teach me how to be a man like he should have. There was a lot of things under the sun that you as a woman couldn't teach me. I needed a man to do that. Yes, you took me to church and things, but life goes beyond church. You don't have to go to church every Sunday to be saved.

Church is in your heart. You hurt me as I was growing up more than my dad did because you would get upset at me. I have seen you and dad fight and be abusive to each other right in front of me. It wasn't like my childhood supposed to be. It was volatile and very abusive, I thought, because a family is supposed to help each other and respect each other, spend time together and show love and not be fighting in front of their kid and family members. It used to hurt me to go home because I didn't want to see you and him fight and argue all the time. For so many years, I felt unloved and mistreated at times, because we were not a family. I use to do things in school just to get back at you and him, but I was only hurting myself, I didn't know that at the time. You used to tell me don't be a "nothing" like your dad, but God don't make nothings. Everybody is something in life." The letter goes on and on.

My first reaction was outrage. I was hurt, pissed. *The nerve, ungratefulness, how dare he!* I was so angry I couldn't get beyond my self-righteousness to see what was said. It was several years later that I realized my son's letter had validity. It was a hard pill to swallow, but the reality was true, and it was heart-wrenching!

Many years ago, I embarked upon a journey that has been a labor of pure grit and sheer determination.

Not having any prior writing experience, but I had a desire to share my story in honesty and sincerity. I'm sure my story represents many whose sons and daughters are incarcerated, on drugs, and have other behavior problems. My sons were bombarded with adult issues at an early age. My personality and behavior goes back to my childhood, with my grandmother and my father. And the cycle was passed on into my marriage. I lost control of myself, by trying to control and change someone else. My two sons mirrored what they were exposed to.

In 2007, Alvin F. Poussiant, M. D., and a known celebrity wrote the book titled *COME ON, PEOPLE* addressing issues in our African-American community. In the book it says, "Homes should be a sanctuary for love and peace, not a hotbed of anger and violence." Unfortunately, I personally can attest to that!

My African American Community: based on statistics, in the United States there are now more than one million black men in jail and that one of every four black males will go to prison in their lifetimes. Locally, in 2011, out of 1364 inmates at Caddo Correctional Center, 1029 were African-American, men and women. Too many of our prospective young Black men have become extinct in today's society, but not in the prisons. Children need a stable home environment, to grow into normal well-adjusted adults, so that they will not grow up believing that prison is a "rite of passage." In the words of the late great Fredrick Douglass; "It is easier to build strong children than repair broken men."

With all due respect...it isn't always the parents fault. This has been MY truth! Hopefully, my story has been a mirror and a blessing for someone else to discover their codependent behaviors and make some changes in their life. So, if I've helped someone else made their discovery of *self* then I have no regrets of exposing my soul. *I believe I've found my purpose.*

Acknowledgments

After a twenty-nine-year journey of dedication to writing my story, no way could I have done it without the help of others. To express myself to all, on these pages would become another book. Those from whom I have received support, encouragement, and prayers, I am very grateful. Patricia Walker Flanagan, and those who edited and sponsored me in my first edition, I have over-whelming gratitude. I would like to bestow a special thanks to my dental hygienist, Lisa Bayne-Woodard, who became my first volunteer sponsor. Lisa, besides being a beautiful young lady, you have such a sweet spirit, and you are an inspiration. I always look forward to my dental visits. Thanks also to my cousin Lonnie Speed, who became a volunteer sponsor, and my cousin Rosetta Singletary Bennett.

Pastor Jacquelyn Richardson Stafford, *Second Chance Temple of Deliverance Church and the Women Ministries*, have been a blessing and a miracle! Pastor Stafford, your prayers and monetary contributions for my success is humbling. My sister in the Lord, your unselfish giving has been mind-blowing. You are truly a Woman of God! Much love and thanks.

A special thanks to Sharon Porter Burford who wrote a poignant Foreword. I would like to express a very special thanks to Martha Holoubek Fitzgerald whose literary expertise gave me confidence to trust the power of my writing, and who coached me pro bono!

Mrs. June Carter Bolch, I met you at the Fitness Center many years ago, and imposed upon you to read my manuscript, which you so graciously obliged, and has been in my corner, since. Mrs. June, your praise reassured me that I had a story worthy of sharing with others. Your insight on how I was trying to tell it was invaluable. I shall never forget you saying, "Now you need to tone this down, some." Thanks Mrs. June, you are a special lady who will forever be in my heart.

To my Spiritual mother and mentor, Rev. Dr. Allie Mae Allen, author of *Ministering to the Whole Child*. Mother Allen, you are by far, the most gracious, elegant, and beautiful lady that I've had the privilege of knowing. Your life exemplifies your love for God and his people, especially those that are less fortunate. Getting acquainted with you that year of 1998, has been such a blessing. I've learned many lessons from you, and your book. Rev. Dr. Allie Mae Bellar Allen—you are AWESOME!

I also acknowledge one of Morning Star's oldest and faithful deacon and "prayer warrior," Deacon Willis Glenn, whose soul stirring, devotional prayers uplifted my "spirits of despair" on many of those Sunday mornings worship experiences. Thanks Deacon Glenn for those uplifting prayers.

I must express my gratitude for the late *Eric Brock*, Historian and author who read my manuscript, gave me feedback, offered suggestions and gave me information. He was one in a million! And I shall never forget him.

I am immensely grateful for Barbara Young at *Hair Gallery Beauty Salon*. Barbara, your enthusiasm, laughter and tears when reading my story gave me the encouragement and inspiration needed to be more creative. You have inspired me more than you could possibly know. Your appreciation for my story has been humbling. Barbara---much love.

A special thanks to my two dearest friends Joyce and Cookie, who have been with me from get-go. Joyce, I definitely believe God placed you in my life during my most vulnerable time. My sister in the Lord, our friendship has sustained over thirty plus years and has grown stronger. You have been there for me even when you've had your illnesses. Your strength and courage have been up against some serious health issues and your faith never wavered. The "prayer warrior" that you are, I have an abundant peace, knowing you're continuously lifting up my sons in prayer... thank you, thank you, thank you!

Joyce King Griffin, you have been a remarkable friend and confidante. I truly love you, my sister!

Cookie my girl, your busy schedule makes me dizzy! I marvel at your relentless commitments. Although you go above and beyond, but still find time to include *Ole boring me*! We speak daily over the phone; checking in. You have been a great supporter, and also my sister in the Lord, whom I love dearly. Your words of encouragement and belief in my book, has meant so much. Ella "Cookie" Cherry, you are a true and loyal friend--- simply the best.

My dear friend Judith Martin Harris, I admire your independent spirit and your bravery. Getting to know you at the Fitness Center has been a joy. On those occasionally luncheons, your laughter always makes it seems I have a sense of humor, saying, "Georgia, you are so funny!" Judy, you've been so supportive of my story. Thanks for accepting me *just as I am*. My Caucasian sister---you're the real deal!

Marjorie Carlson Bowen and Suzanne McCawley Burford, thanks for your support. In my intrusiveness, you've never failed to critique those few pages that I have sprang upon the two of you, unexpectedly. My two lovely and vivacious twins, your kindness and affection shown to me have been none less than remarkable. I feel the love! It is very much reciprocated. Thanks for allowing me to become part of your family; entrusting me to baby-sit your kids. I always treasure those hours, and it is an honor and a privilege.

Suzanne and Porter, you have an incredible love story. Through adversities your love for each other persevered and became stronger than ever. Porter, you have such a giving spirit. I am incredibly appreciative---by your generosity. It is beyond belief. John Porter Burford, you're the CAT'S-MEOW!

Thanks to my pastor, Theron Jackson, author of *Never Be Nothing* whose book inspires and motivates young Black males into becoming a positive influence in today's society. Rev. Dr. Theron J. Jackson thanks for your generosity! It was very much appreciated.

Thanks to Noel Memorial Library Archives and Special Collections, Louisiana State University in Shreveport, for the collected information of George D'Artois.

Much appreciation goes to Rev. Dr. Harry Blake. Thanks for allowing me to be creative with small snippets of events that occurred in your life during that special period of time. Realizing, I am by no means qualified to write about all those dangerous events that you and others encountered in fighting for equality and justice. Pastor Blake, the African American Community owes you and all those other local Civil Rights Activists a debt of gratitude for your sacrifices made in the late 50s and 60s for equal rights. Your bravery will never be forgotten.

To my sister Deborah English Richmond, thank you for patiently teaching me how to use the computer. It's not easy, having to train someone struck in the twentieth century. Surely I worked your nerves! But baby-sis, we did it! Thank you for always being there for me. I love you!

Becoming a member of WK Fitness Center in 1997 had many benefits. Much later in the early 2000s, it allowed me to meet and forge a lasting friendship with one of the young trainer who is a minister, and a Caucasian, whom I've bonded with he and his family. He's been such a blessing in my life. I call him "my Jesus friend." Thank you, Currie Godfrey, for showing kindness to this senior citizen! We build bridges!

Lastly, I would like to give a special thanks to Hayden, who provided the final editing to my book. In January 2018, I was so blessed to have her fussed over my grammar and fine-tuned each chapter. She provided erroneous improvements. Hayden Bean, thank you for freely investing your time toward helping me with my project. You are a beautiful, kind, talented, gifted, and incredibly smart young 9th grader.

A Heart-felt Appreciation

I would be remiss not to give appreciation to my "Jesus friend" Currie Godfrey and his wife Elizabeth for starting the GoFundMe page. As a result, I was able to raise funds for the printing of my self-published book. I am extending heart-felt gratitude for all those that contributed to the fundraiser! Thank you so much for believing in my story and making this a reality.

I especially thank my dentist, Dr. Frank, who after reading a copy, bought 5 books and several months later, he voluntarily wrote out a check for the printing of 20 books of which he only kept four. What an encouragement for me, the author! Thank you, Dr. Frank Gaensehals. Never shall I forget your generosity.

Mr. Van Winn! I can't say enough about how blessed I am to have met you many years ago at the fitness center. You are such an amazing elderly young man! Thank you for your contribution! You are a giving and caring gentleman.

Patrick & Shanna Durr, what a blessing you've been also! Thank you from the bottom of my heart.

There are many other contributors to thank! Here are their names:

Julie Nix, Martha Taylor, Joshua Fuller, Nell Sisson, Joey Vallot, Hannah Barnett, Tim Smith, Dapheni Franklin, Elizabeth Godfrey, Suzanne Burford, Shelton O. Bryant, Ida Hall, Lorita Brooks, Marjorie Bowen, and Dympha Ahmed.

Last said: I, Maple Sudds Bernard, give thanks and appreciation for every one that has supported and encouraged me in the final phase of this journey!

THOUGHT PROVOKING
QUESTIONS FOR DISCUSSION

1. In the Introduction, Georgann writes, "a codependent is one who has let another person's behavior affect him or her, and who is obsessed with controlling that person's behavior. Do you think Georgann's codependency behaviors came about from her childhood when she would go searching for her father on those Friday nights?

2. As a teenager, Georgann vowed never to marry a man like her father. Can you compare and contrast the similarities of Luke and George's behavior?

3. How much of an influence did Olivia play in her granddaughter's life by telling her that "a man is gonna be a man, but it is left to the woman to be the *best wife* that she can be?"

4. Sometimes it takes a jolting experience to make one face reality. Why do you think it climaxed to Jeff's behavior with Dorothy's gun and Luke's involvement for Georgann's ultimate decision to finally end her marriage?

5. Do you feel that Georgann's devotion to Christianity gave her the un-canny notion that she had the capability of helping Luke to change his behavior? Do you feel that Luke changed Georgann's behavior?

6. If Jeff and Carl had been provided a normal, safe, healthy and secure environment, do you feel that their lives would still have turned out so destructive? What part does genetics have in a person's behavior compared to learned behavior?

7. Do you think Georgann would have fared better with Jeff and Carl if she had became a single parent?

8. What do you think about Joyce and Georgann's friendship? Could Joyce have been used as a vessel to help Georgann get through those difficult times and to help strengthen her faith? What about Brother Henry? Do you think that he also was a vessel used to help Georgann? If so, explain why.

9. When Jeff returned home and apologized to his mother, do you feel that Georgann did the

right thing by not allowing him to live with her? What would you have done?

10. Do you think Georgann could have done more to help her twenty-one-year old son, Carl?

11. Do you feel that Georgann's story is a typical black story? Do you believe our children lives mirror their environment? Was Luke right when he told Georgann in essence, that his behavior had no affect on Jeff, due to the fact that Luke had seen children whose parents were alcoholics make something out of themselves... did Luke make a point? How do some children whose situations are far worse than others overcome adversities?

12. Guilt can hold one hostage and keep one in bondage. Things one should have done and said, but didn't, may leave one with a lifetime of regret. What age do you feel adult children should take responsibility and be accountable for their life in spite of their dire circumstances?

13. Do you think that it was divine intervention which prevented Luke from taking Georgann's

life when he had the knife at her throat? Or was Luke not violent as he projected?

14. Often times we make decisions that are not wise, and "the choices we make dictate the life we live." Georgann had trials upon trials but she persevered. Why you think God gave Georgann her personality?

15. Has Georgann's story been an eye-opener to you? If your life had been similar, would you be willing to be so earnest and open in sharing your life story if it could help others? Has her story influenced you to make any changes in your own life?

BIO

Maple Sudds Bernard, aka Georgann. Born in 1944 to Essie Dell Sudds and George Written. She is a native of Shreveport, La., reared in the community of Mooretown by her Grandmother, Olivia Singletary Written and father George. A member of Morning Star Missionary Baptist Church, a 1962 member of the first graduating class of the former Bethune Junior and Senior High School. A 1995 retired AT&T Employee. Contact: 318-635-6166 (home) 318-564-9008.

CPSIA information can be obtained
at www.ICGtesting.com
Printed in the USA
BVHW070931010619
549894BV00001B/17/P